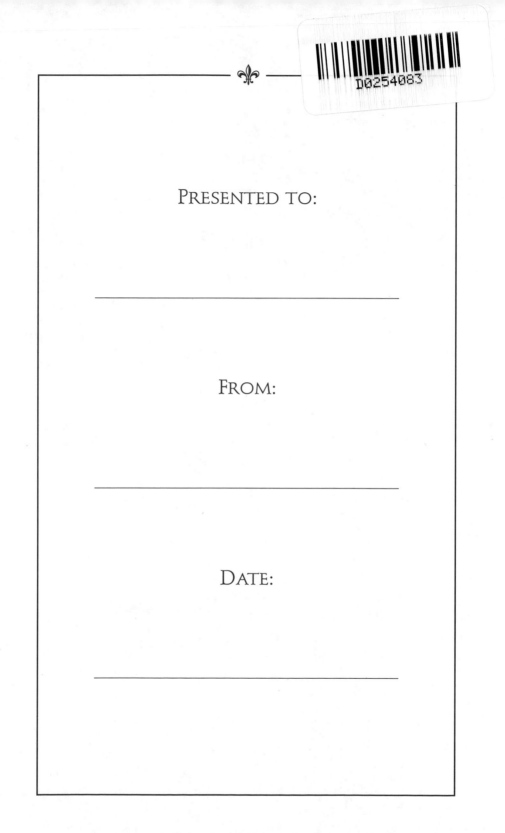

PRESENTED TO:

_____

FROM:

_____

DATE:

_____

YOU CAN BE A
WORLD CHANGER

101 Stories of People Who Made a Difference . . .
and You Can Too!

07 06 05 04 03   10 9 8 7 6 5 4 3 2 1

You Can Be a World Changer:
101 Stories of People Who Made a Difference . . . and You Can Too!
ISBN 1-56292-807-4
Copyright © 2003 by Honor Books
An Imprint of Cook Communications Ministries
4050 Lee Vance View
Colorado Springs, Colorado 80918

Manuscript prepared by W. B. Freeman Concepts, Inc., Tulsa, Oklahoma.

INTRODUCTION

*"Whatever things were rightly said among
all men, are the property of us Christians."*
Justin Martyr (B. 100; D. 165)

Want to live a life that makes a difference? Great world changers often state that the examples from the past inspired their own reach for excellence. So one way for you to begin is to make yourself familiar with the character qualities of those people you admire who have already made a difference in the world.

The Apostle Paul stated that when people who don't know God's law do what is right naturally, they show that principles for living a life that God approves are written already on their hearts. (See Romans 2:14-15.) This truth also gives us the freedom to learn from great people of all backgrounds who follow the world-changing principles that God wrote on their hearts. Within the pages of *You Can Be a World Changer* you will find a collection of small biographical sketches for your encouragement and inspiration followed by a World-Changer Principle drawn from each life.

Great people of faith like Dietrich Bonhoeffer, Corrie ten Boom, and Martin Luther King will show you the way to reach beyond great difficulties to maintain your faith and integrity as you make a difference in your world. People of other backgrounds like Elie Wiesel, Itzak Perlman, and John Wayne will provide examples of important character qualities that you will want to nurture in your own life as you become a person who makes a positive difference in the world. However, not all the names in this book will be ones you readily recognize. You will also learn about people like Anna Leonowens, Oseola McCarty, and Raoul Wallenberg, who changed their communities and their world. Their lives will inspire you to become the kind of person who changes your world too.

Want to make a difference? Learn from those who changed the world. Then move out to change your community and your world— live a life that makes a difference!

Contents

ABRAHAM AND SARAH
(circa 2000 B. C.—circa 1825 B. C.)

"Lives of Genuine Faith"

Few people have given up as much—or gained as much—as Abram and Sarah, considered the patriarch and matriarch of the Hebrew people.

Born in the renowned Mesopotamian city of Ur, the center of Sumerian culture, Abram rejected the polytheism of his culture and became the first known person in world literature to openly advocate and teach the existence of "one God." Following God's command to him to "get up and get out" of Mesopotamia, Abram left Ur and traveled well-established trade routes to Haran, and then after the death of his father, he entered Canaan. For the next hundred years, he lived a nomadic life in the land he believed God had promised to him and his descendants. His travels took him from Dan in the north to Egypt in the south, with many of his years in Canaan spent at Hebron.

The bulk of the Hebrew scriptures is the story of God's work in and through Abram and his descendants. The original story of creation and the account of Noah and the great flood are stories told from the perspective of Abram's faith and lineage. His role in the Old Testament is couched in terms of covenant—a binding statement of relationship between God and a person. The covenant includes a two-fold blessing of land and children. Abram's acceptance of God's covenant relationship prompted his name change from Abram to Abraham, which means "father of a multitude," and his wife's name from Sarai to Sarah, which means "princess."

Both the Old Testament and the New Testament emphasize Abraham's faith in God. His faith was rewarded not only with vast flocks and herds, but also with a miracle son, Isaac, born to his wife Sarah long past normal childbearing years. He was also the father of Ishmael, born to Sarah's servant Hagar. Isaac, in turn, bore Esau and Jacob, from whom the Israelites descended. Ishmael became the father of many of the Arab tribes. After Sarah's death, Abraham took Keturah as his concubine, and she bore him six sons who also became leaders of Arab tribes, notably Midian. He died at age 175 and was buried by the side of Sarah in Machpelah.

Perhaps at no time was Abraham's faith tested more strongly than at the time God called him to sacrifice his beloved son, Isaac. Abraham responded with faith and obedience, and at the last moment, Isaac's life was spared by God, who provided a ram in a thicket to take his place.

Known as a man of wisdom, piety, and prayer, Abraham interceded for Abimelech and on behalf of Sodom and Gomorrah.

Abraham established a pattern of living that his descendants might follow the Lord explicitly and with faith. He is thus called the "father of all who believe" by the apostle Paul in a letter to Roman Christians (see Romans 4:11). Abraham is also called the "friend of God" repeatedly in the Scriptures, a title given to no one else in history. Abraham's greatness comes from his willingness to believe in God's goodness and trustworthiness against all evidence to the contrary. As a result, God blessed Abraham and changed the world through Him.[1]

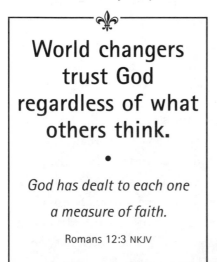

❖

World changers trust God regardless of what others think.

•

God has dealt to each one a measure of faith.

Romans 12:3 NKJV

Roald Engebreth Gravning Amundsen

(1872–1928)

"The Last Great Viking Explorer"

When the Norwegian explorer Fridtjof Nansen did something no person had attempted—crossing the polar ice cap on skis and with dog-drawn sledges—Roald Amundsen was among those who cheered his homecoming in Norway. Nansen's feat came on the heels of Amundsen's reading a book about the English Arctic explorer Sir John Franklin. Together, the two experiences marked the beginning of Amundsen's life goal: to travel the Arctic.

Roald Amundsen seemed born to the sea. His father amassed a fortune as a ship skipper, and with Amundsen's uncles, owned thirty ships. His mother, however, desired for her youngest of four sons to become a medical doctor. Out of respect for his mother and because she held the purse strings of the family after his father's death, Roald did attend medical school. He read more reports of the world's polar explorers, however, than medical books, and after his mother's death, he pursued with single-minded focus his dreams of polar expeditions.

In preparation for the Arctic wastelands, he practiced skiing in the mountains of western Norway; studied astronomy, map reading, and surveying; and spent time at sea earning his Mate's and then Master's certificates. He was also part of an expedition to Antarctica in 1897.

The ship became icebound, and many on board died, became ill, or went insane—but Amundsen thrived on the experience. He and a ship-mate invented a new type of tent designed to withstand fierce Antarctic windstorms. After this experience, Amundsen returned to Norway ready to make his own expedition—he chose as his challenge the first traversing of the Northwest Passage.

Four years later, Amundsen set sail in a twenty-nine-year-old sloop that had been used for herring fishing and was powered by a kerosene motor. They became ice-locked for two years, but rather than pursue an overland exit, Amundsen remained in the area for two reasons: he conducted definitive scientific studies that proved the variability of the Magnetic North Pole, and he learned valuable techniques from the Eskimos about life in the Arctic. His journey through the Northwest Passage was completed in August of 1905.

Two years later, Amundsen took Nansen's ship, Fram, on an expedition to reach the South Pole. The expedition turned into a race with British explorer Robert Falcon Scott. In the end, Amundsen and five of his men reached the South Pole a full month before Scott did. The skills he had learned from the Eskimos had made the difference.

In 1926, Amundsen made his trip to the North Pole in an airship built and piloted by Italian engineer Umberto Nobile. He became the first person in history to reach both poles. Two years later, when word reached him that Nobile had crashed into the Arctic waters, Amundsen set out in an effort to locate and rescue him. His "flying

> **World changers pursue their dreams with single-minded focus and determination.**
>
> •
>
> *Whatever you do,*
>
> *do it heartily.*
>
> Colossians 3:23 NKJV

boat" was seen heading into a fog bank along the northwestern horizon, but where it went down, no one knows. As a young man, Roald Amundsen had said that he wanted to die as the explorer Franklin had, "not in a burning desert but in the frosty North." His death was just that.[2]

Brother Andrew
(1928)

❧

"He Refused To Be Shut Out By Communism"

Brother Andrew, who refuses to reveal his last name, has been a champion of the suffering Church around the world for nearly fifty years. While in his twenties, he began to smuggle desperately desired Bibles to Christians behind the Iron Curtain, usually hiding them in the back seat of a beat-up Volkswagen Beetle. He later began an organization to train others in Bible-smuggling techniques. He once said, "Show me a closed door, and I will tell you how you can get in. I won't, however, promise you a way to get out."

The fall of communism in Europe did not end his work. His Open Door ministry still maintains offices in some twenty countries and has two hundred full-time workers. He has said, "Communism proclaimed that there is no God, which is stupid and schizophrenic, because they say there is no God, and then they fight Him. The challenge now is . . . the challenge of 'Who is God?' Islam confronts us with that question."

When his beloved older brother Bas lay dying of tuberculosis, eleven-year-old Andrew was determined that "if Bas was going to die, then I wanted to die too." He seemed to have been unfazed by the prospect of dying since he was a child. He threw himself on his brother and kissed him repeatedly in an attempt to contract the disease. His attempt failed. When the Germans bombed an airstrip close to his home on his twelfth birthday, he engaged in a dangerous one-boy war when he took the family's highly valued sugar ration and dumped it into the gas tank of a

German vehicle. He joined the army at age seventeen and became a tank driver, one of the most dangerous assignments in World War II.

While on a paramilitary assignment to Indonesia after the war, he seemed to hear God calling to him with the same words Moses spoke, "Let My people go." He returned to Europe to attend a missionary school in Glasgow, Scotland, and he made his first trip behind the Iron Curtain in 1955. Shortly thereafter he articulated his personal mandate: "We find out what a church needs . . . we come back and supply it."

The European communists could not shut out Brother Andrew, but a book about his work, *God's Smuggler*, did. The book sold 10 million copies in twenty-seven languages, but its success raised his personal profile to a dangerous level. On the positive side, the book inspired others to continue his work, and it freed Brother Andrew to turn his attention to other areas of the world still closed to the Gospel.

His current efforts include taking Bibles and Christian materials into China, Cuba, Vietnam, Islamic nations in Africa, and remote areas of Latin America. He has sponsored prayer campaigns and inter-denominational congresses for Christian leaders. He continues to lead an effort to distribute Bibles to school children in the former Soviet Union provinces. In a recent year, his organization trained tens of thousands of pastors and lay leaders and distributed more than a million Bibles and New Testaments, as well as more than a million copies of the Gospels, spiritual books, and other forms of Christian literature.[3]

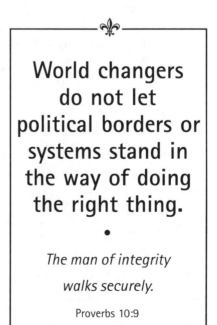

World changers do not let political borders or systems stand in the way of doing the right thing.

•

The man of integrity

walks securely.

Proverbs 10:9

Neil Armstrong
(1930)

❧

"He Was The First Man To Set Foot On The Moon"

From the time he was a boy, Neil Armstrong wanted to fly. He took his first airplane ride when he was six years old and began to build model airplanes at age nine. As a teenager, he got a job after school to earn money for flying lessons, and on his sixteenth birthday, two years after he began taking lessons, he passed his flying test and became a pilot.

In an attempt to study aeronautical engineering, Armstrong enrolled in Purdue University; but the Korean War began about the same time. Armstrong became a fighter pilot in the United States Navy and flew seventy-eight combat flights in his three years in Korea. He was shot down behind enemy lines on one flight; and on another, flew a damaged plane to safe landing on an aircraft carrier. He was awarded three Air Medals.

He was asked to become a test pilot after he left the Navy and had finished his degree at Purdue as a result of his well known piloting skills. As a test pilot, many of the planes he flew had never been flown before. One such plane was the *X-15*—part airplane and part rocket. In flying the *X-15*, Armstrong flew 3,989 miles an hour and as high as thirty-eight miles above the earth's surface. No other airplane had ever flown as fast or as high.

Armstrong became part of NASA in the 1960s with the start of the *Gemini* program. In 1966, he was launched into space for the first time in *Gemini 8*. The mission was intended to connect the *Gemini 8* craft with another spacecraft; but during a test hookup, the two spacecraft began to tumble out of control. Armstrong made quick decisions that allowed the craft to return safely to earth.

While testing a Lunar Landing Research Vehicle at an air base in Houston in 1968, Armstrong nearly lost his life. He was able to pull the eject handle and parachute to safety just moments before the LLRV crashed into the ground. He later said, "The only damage to me was that I bit my tongue."

In 1969, Armstrong was aboard *Apollo 11* with astronauts Edwin "Buzz" Aldrin Jr. and Michael Collins as it was launched at Cape Canaveral, Florida. Three days later, the men found themselves in an orbit around the moon, 240,000 miles from the earth.

On July 20, 1969, Armstrong and Aldrin flew the landing craft *Eagle* away from the *Apollo 11* command module. After navigating his way around an area covered with large rocks, Armstrong found a safe place for the lunar module to land. As he brought the craft to rest on the moon's surface, he radioed back a simple message, "Tranquillity Base here. The *Eagle* has landed."

After several hours of preparation, Armstrong opened the *Eagle*

> # World changers are willing to undertake what others have never done.
>
> •
>
> *The steps of a good man are ordered by the LORD, And He delights in his way.*
>
> Psalm 37:23 NKJV

17

door, climbed slowly down a ladder, and set foot on the moon. Millions around the world applauded. Armstrong's statement upon touching the moon's surface has been echoed through the decades, "That's one small step for man, one giant leap for mankind." He and Aldrin left a message on the moon that was signed by the three astronauts and President Richard Nixon. It read, "Here men from the planet earth first set foot upon the moon July 1969, A.D. We came in peace for all mankind."[4]

Arthur Ashe
(1943–1993)

❦

"He Gave A New Face And A New Demeanor To Tennis"

Arthur Ashe lived a life of achievement coupled with discipline. After his mother's death when he was six years old, he grew up in a home strictly regimented by his father. He graduated with honors from college, where he first studied architecture but later switched to business administration so he would have more time for tennis. All his life, he was a shrewd businessman with a great capacity to enjoy both the "business of his sport" and the "sport of business." He became an international tennis star and was the top-ranked men's player in the world in 1975. He became the first black to break into the "all white world" of tennis.

Early tennis teachers required Ashe to have impeccable manners on the court so that whites could never accuse him of meanness. He once wrote, "I want to be seen as fair and honest, trustworthy, kind, calm, and polite." His favorite piece of advice for children was, "Don't do anything you couldn't tell your mother about." At times he was accused of being cold or aloof, but Ashe preferred the term "controlled." He strongly believed a certain amount of detachment was necessary to be a good tennis player in control of his game. Rather than respond in anger to the bigotry he experienced as a black tennis player, he adopted an attitude of "Well, I'll show them."

The only time Ashe was known to lose his temper was at a 1975 tournament in Sweden. His opponent's racial taunts became unbearable, and he walked off the court in protest, defaulting that match rather than responding in anger in public. Even given this opponent's bad behavior, Ashe continued to consider the man a friend, and he invited him to his wedding.

At a benefit for the United Negro College Fund, Ashe met his wife, when she asked if she could take photos of him. He married photographer Jeanne Moutoussamy, who later gave birth to their daughter Camera. He was a devoted father to his daughter. With Camera, he regularly visited poor families on Christmas Day to give away toys, including a few of Camera's new ones. He was a man who required very little quantity in personal luxury but chose maximum quality. At the time of his death, he owned only five suits and five pairs of shoes.

As an activist in the fight against social injustices, he was even willing to be arrested during protests. He also sought to work "within the system" and served on a number of corporate boards. After heart surgery in 1983, he contracted AIDS from a tainted blood transfusion. His transfusion had come just two years before blood was routinely tested for HIV. Rather than withdraw from public life after his diagnosis, he continued to accept speaking engagements to publicize the realities of AIDS. He addressed the United Nations on World AIDS Day in 1992, just months before his death. He once said that while he had great joy in being a professional athlete, "the purest joy in life comes from trying to help others."

Much of Ashe's life was riddled with unfairness, but he rose above injustices and bad breaks with a true gentleman's attitude.[5]

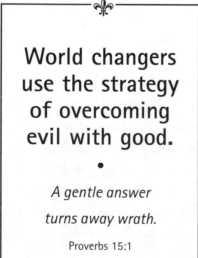

World changers use the strategy of overcoming evil with good.

•

A gentle answer turns away wrath.

Proverbs 15:1

JOHANN SEBASTIAN BACH
(1685–1750)

❧

"A Master Of Masters"

It seemed natural that Johann Sebastian Bach should follow in the family tradition. His ancestors had been distinguished musicians for generations, and he was trained in music from early childhood. He secured his first paying job as a violinist at the Weimar court when he was still a teenager. He later held several organ and choir positions. In 1723, he became music director of the two main churches at Leipzig, where he remained until his death.

Johann Sebastian Bach wrote many of his compositions so that he might perform original music at the Leipzig churches each week. He was far more than a church organist, however. Bach composed for the piano, stringed instruments, and the human voice. His vocal works—including oratorios, masses, and cantatas—are considered by many to be among the greatest choral pieces ever written, and the vast majority of them based on biblical themes. Several of his oratorios are still performed around the world at Easter and Christmas.

Hailed as the greatest organist of his time, Bach's preludes and fugues for organ are standard organ music even today. Bach developed a new system of fingering, which had great influence on modern piano playing, and *The Well-tempered Clavichord* has been in use for more than 250 years. Bach himself had little systematic training. What he had learned from his family came through hearing, copying, imitating, and experimenting. He spent years attempting to educate himself in musical technique and then even more years attempting to pass on what he had learned.

On one occasion, Bach was asked to appraise his own life's work. He said simply, "I worked hard." The fact is, no composer worked harder. After his death, librarians took forty-six years to gather and publish all his work—the result was a collection that filled sixty large volumes. One modern-day music copyist estimated that seventy years of diligent work would be required to copy all of Bach's work by hand, which is how Bach wrote them.

For all of his greatness in music, Bach received little tangible reward. He had a low salary, and his living conditions were once described as "dark, constricted, cold, and unsanitary." Six of his first eight children died before reaching adulthood, and his rector often humiliated him in public. Bach, however, did not live for reward. As one musician stated, "He lived but to worship God and to write music."

World changers seek to perfect their natural gifts and to pass on what they learn.

•

*Never tire of doing
what is right.*

2 Thessalonians 3:13

Bach has been called the first of the great German musicians and the "master of masters" because his works inspired so many of the famous musicians who followed him, including Mozart, Beethoven, Mendelssohn, Schumann, Chopin, Liszt, Rubinstein, and Wagner. In addition to his work as a musician and composer, Bach also taught a class of boys in music and Latin in Leipzig. The heritage he passed on included a musical "inheritance" to his children. He was the father of twenty children, eleven of whom became musicians.[6]

CLARA BARTON
(1821–1912)

❧

"The Angel Of The Battlefield"

"I don't know how long it has been since my ear has been free from the roll of a drum," Clara wrote her father. "It is the music I sleep by, and I love it."

Although she was timid, Clara Barton seemed to have two passions from the time she was a child—a desire to enlist in the military, which was impossible for her as a woman, and a desire to help others. Her first experience in "helping" came when she was eleven. For two years, she nursed her brother David, who was injured in a fall. Later, during a smallpox epidemic, she nursed her neighbors. Clara, however, did not pursue a career in nursing. Rather, she became a teacher at age fifteen and taught for eighteen years. She began a school for poor children of sawmill workers in Massachusetts and later founded a public school in Bordentown, New Jersey. Her school grew to 600 students in two years, at which time the board selected a man to run it, saying "the job was too important for a woman to hold." Clara promptly resigned and in anger, moved to Washington, D. C., where she took a job in the Patent Office.

From childhood, Clara had idolized her father, a soldier who taught her to be a superb horsewoman and a dead shot with a revolver. She was strong physically and could handle a saw and a hammer, as well as a wagon team. When the Civil War broke out, it seemed only natural for her to get involved. She advertised for food and medical supplies for the wounded and then organized their distribution. Her efforts took her and her mule-trains of supplies to the front lines. She refused to allow the Army to have any control over her activities, thus sidestepping bureaucratic delays. She received no government financial backing but rather, raised virtually all of her operational funds from private donors. In addition to her supply-line work, she was the supervisor of nurses at a field hospital. Her efforts opened the way for other women to serve in battlefield hospitals.

After the war ended, Barton organized a search for missing soldiers and was able to locate more than 22,000 missing men in four years. Four years later, she went to Europe and became involved there with the International Red Cross. In 1881, she and several friends founded the American National Red Cross Society, and Barton served as president. Her goal differed slightly from that of the international group— Barton believed the Red Cross should not only help wounded soldiers but also victims of natural disasters. Only months after the Society was established, it sent volunteers and more than $80,000 in supplies to an area of Michigan devastated by a forest fire.

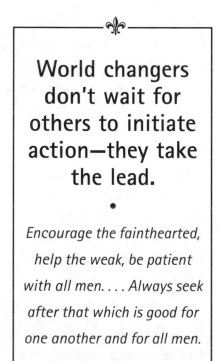

World changers don't wait for others to initiate action—they take the lead.

•

Encourage the fainthearted, help the weak, be patient with all men. . . . Always seek after that which is good for one another and for all men.

2 Thessalonians 5:14–15 NASB

Barton worked for twelve years to convince the United States Government to officially join the International Red Cross, but she eventually succeeded. Her efforts at marshaling forces to aid in disasters were so effective in the United States that the International Red Cross eventually adopted a similar stance, expanding its purpose to the meeting of needs that were not related to the battlefield.

In spite of her own frail health, Clara Barton worked tirelessly in her Red Cross role until she was in her nineties.[7]

LUDWIG VAN BEETHOVEN
(1770–1827)

❧

"He Continued To Hear What Was Important"

What word do you use to describe a musician who is an accomplished pianist by the age of ten and whose compositions are published by age thirteen? What word befits a musician who is a paid professional organist at eleven and a member of the court musical staff at thirteen? Virtuoso! It is a word often associated with Ludwig van Beethoven.

What few do not know is the tragic side of Beethoven's early years. As a black-haired, swarthy-complexioned, pockmarked youngster, Beethoven was taunted by name-callers in his home along the Rhine River, an area of blond children. When his alcoholic father discovered his talent, he determined that the young Ludwig would become his financial support, and he insisted that Ludwig become a slave to the keyboard. Herr Pfeiffer, a talented musician who was also an alcoholic, became Ludwig's live-in teacher, and thus, at age nine Ludwig had two difficult taskmasters to please. Beethoven later said that he could recall no moments of childhood happiness. His life had been one of work, tears, beatings, lessons, and angry tirades from his father. Although she was gentle and understanding, his mother was overworked and afraid of life—her greatest encouragement to Beethoven was this advice: "Be strong, my son. Be strong. Some day you will be great."

As a young man, Beethoven's brilliance at the keyboard won him the applause of Vienna, praise from Mozart, and Haydn as a teacher.

His compositions were not as well received since they broke the "rules" of music in his day. His impatience with high society was not forgiven. And all the while, Beethoven struggled against yet another unseen enemy: deafness.

Beethoven first began to lose his hearing in his twenties, and by his late forties, he was totally deaf. He declared, however, "I will grapple with Fate; it shall never drag me down." When he could no longer play in public because of his deafness, he threw all of his energies into composing. He withdrew to a great extent from society, and in spite of illness—near constant gout and growing rheumatism—he continued to say to himself, "Courage! . . . My spirit shall rule." His years of deafness became his most prolific.

In all, Beethoven composed nine symphonies, thirty-two piano sonatas, five piano concertos, ten sonatas for the piano and violin, a series of string quartets, vocal music, theater music, and much more. His compositions greatly influenced later composers such as Brahms, Wagner, Schubert, and Tchaikovsky. He is credited with expanding the size of orchestras, lengthening symphonies, placing increasing value on the piano, and marking the transition from classical to romantic styles of music.

Near death, Beethoven knew that the world had not understood him or his music, but with a happy smile on his face, he whispered, "I shall hear in Heaven."[8]

> # World changers refuse to allow outer circumstances to stop the expression of their God-given talents.
>
> •
>
> *I have learned in whatever state I am, to be content.*
>
> Philippians 4:11 NKJV

ALEXANDER GRAHAM BELL
(1847-1922)

⚜

"He Gave The World A New Way To Communicate"

Alexander Graham Bell grew up in a world of sound. His father was an expert in vocal physiology, speech correction, and teaching the deaf. Although Alexander had only a few years of formal schooling, he was well-educated by his family and himself; and he became an expert in his father's system of "visible speech."

Born in Scotland, he moved to Boston when he was twenty-four years old and became a professor of vocal physiology at Boston University. Four years later, he made the discoveries that led to his invention of the telephone. Few inventions have been more widely used or have had such a tremendous impact on everyday life.

What most people do not know is that Bell was not the first to experiment with a "talking device." Much research was being done in the field. A German school teacher named Reis developed a device that could carry whistling and humming sounds, but not the human voice. Bell discovered that a small screw that controlled the electrodes on Reis's invention needed to be adjusted one-thousandth of an inch. When he turned the screw this minute amount, he was able to transmit speech loud and clear. Bell also barely made it to the patent office first with his discovery. Elisha Gray filed a patent claim for a device very similar to Bell's on the very same day in February 1876, only at a slightly later hour!

Bell was not only an inventor, but also a promoter. He displayed his telephone at the Centennial Exposition in Philadelphia in 1876 and won an award for it. When Western Union Telegraph Company declined to purchase the invention for an asking price of $100,000, Bell and several business associates decided to form a company of their own. In July 1877, they formed the forerunner of today's American Telephone and Telegraph Company (AT&T). The telephone met with prompt and enormous commercial success.

Somewhat ironically, Bell and his wife—who together owned about fifteen percent of the company's shares—sold the majority of their stock at an average price of only $250 a share because Mrs. Bell feared that the stock would never go higher. Just a few months later, the average price was $1,000 a share. Even so, by 1883 the Bells were millionaires.

Bell used his wealth to continue to pursue research activities, including the perfection of the telephone. By 1915, he had developed the device so that a conversation could be carried on between New York and San Francisco. He also invented several other devices: the photophone (which conveyed sounds by vibrating beams of light), the graphophone (which was the forerunner to the phonograph), and the telephone probe (which could detect bullets in the human body). His interests were varied, but he never abandoned his foremost goal, which was always to help the deaf. He wrote numerous articles on the education of the deaf and was considered a highly respected authority on the subject. His wife, in fact, was a deaf girl whom he had formerly tutored.[9]

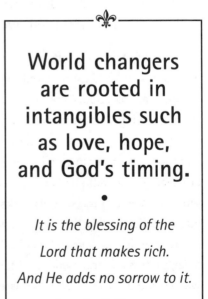

World changers are rooted in intangibles such as love, hope, and God's timing.

•

It is the blessing of the Lord that makes rich. And He adds no sorrow to it.

Proverbs 10:22 NASB

ELIZABETH BLACKWELL
(1821–1910)

❧

"The First Woman Doctor"

The day that Elizabeth went to visit a dying friend was a day that changed her life. Her friend told her with a long sigh that if she had only been treated by a "lady doctor," she might not be dying. The woman had been too ashamed to mention her internal problems to a man, and by the time she finally did seek treatment, it was too late. Elizabeth walked away from her bedside with tears and a mission for her life.

Although Elizabeth's family had once been wealthy, they had run into hard times and had immigrated to the United States when Elizabeth was eleven years old. Soon after, her father died, and Elizabeth spent her teen years knowing what it meant to be "needy." She had a deep compassion for others, and her compassion drove her to prepare for medical training. She took a job teaching, and at night she read medical books. When Elizabeth finally felt she had learned enough to enter medical school, she wrote to twenty-nine schools seeking admission. Most didn't reply, and others replied rudely that women were not meant to be doctors. Finally, a small medical college in New York put her admission to a vote of the dean, professors, and students. After several hours of debate, Elizabeth was accepted. In 1849, she graduated at the top of her class, the first woman to receive a medical degree in the United States.

As difficult as it had been for Elizabeth to get into medical school, it was more difficult for her to find a job. She finally was accepted as a *nursing* apprentice at a maternity hospital in France. There, she contracted an infection in caring for a sick baby and lost the sight of one eye. Her hopes for a career as a surgeon were ruled out, but she still hoped to work as a physician. A prestigious hospital in London eventually accepted her for a graduate position. After two years in Europe, she returned to the United States and advertised: "Miss Elizabeth Blackwell, M.D. . . . has just opened an office at Number 44, University Place, and is prepared to practice in every department of her profession." She received three letters from women asking her to call on them at their homes.

When Elizabeth sought work at a large clinic, she was rejected with the reply: "Found your own dispensary." She snapped back, "I will!" She rented the basement room of a Sunday school, ran ads in newspapers, and gave lectures about healthcare only for women. Many who attended her lectures became patients.

Elizabeth had helped her younger sister Emily attend medical school and become a surgeon. Together, they worked in the clinic. They saw three hundred patients their first year and three thousand patients the second year. Over the next ninety years, more than a million patients were seen at the clinic Elizabeth founded.

She also wrote numerous articles and gave countless speeches to women about nutrition, the need for clean air and exercise, and the importance of keeping one's body and house clean. She helped found and develop the curriculum for both a nursing school and a women's medical college, where she was a professor of "hygiene." She worked until her death at age eighty-nine, with a firm belief: "Each soul must answer to its Maker, so I work on in joyful faith."[10]

> **World changers pursue a life of service to others rather than a self-serving life of money, fame, or glory.**
>
> •
>
> *O Lord, surely I am*
> *Your servant.*
>
> Psalm 116:16 NASB

DIETRICH BONHOEFFER
(1906–1945)

"He Was Willing To Give Up His Life
For What He Believed"

Dietrich Bonhoeffer seemed destined from birth to a life of privilege and academics. The son of a distinguished family, he received his doctorate in theology at the University of Berlin. He taught in Berlin for several years as a Lutheran theologian.

A student pastorate in Barcelona broadened Bonhoeffer's view of the world through study in the United States and attendance at a Cambridge conference of the World Alliance for Promoting International Friendship through the Churches. He became the Youth Secretary for the latter organization in Germany and Central Europe and began to speak on matters of doctrine and heresy in which he felt the church had betrayed Christ, including the treatment of Jews and false church government in his homeland of Germany.

From 1933 on, Bonhoeffer openly criticized the Hitler regime. He categorically rejected the "Aryan clauses" that removed Jews from public offices and church posts and became very active in the Confessing Church, a group of pastors who refused to cooperate with Nazism. Bonhoeffer worked in alternative schools established by the Confessing Church. When the Nazis closed those schools, he continued to teach in an underground "collective pastorate" program.

A teaching position Bonhoeffer accepted at Union Theological Seminary in New York in 1939 would have allowed him to bypass World War II, but he chose to return home. With war imminent, he felt responsible for ministering to German Christians.

In 1940, after the Nazis banned Bonhoeffer from preaching, his brother-in-law secured a job for him on the staff of military intelligence *(Abwehr)*. He was allowed to travel abroad and gather news, pass on information about the progress of the German resistance movement, and use his ecumenical ties to gain credibility in the West for a planned overthrow of Hitler. He served as a courier in delicate but unsuccessful overtures to the British government. The work of the *Abwehr* in planning the overthrow of Hitler was discovered, and Bonhoeffer and others were arrested in April 1943. He spent eighteen months in Tegel military prison in Berlin. In 1944, he was moved to a Gestapo prison in Berlin, and there he weathered the Allied bombing of the city. In February 1945, he was transferred to Buchenwald concentration camp and in April to Flossenburg camp. There, he was officially labeled an *Abwehr* agent. He and five others were court-martialed and subjected to an all-night "trial" in the laundry house. The next morning, April 9, 1945, the men were executed by hanging.

Bonhoeffer's two most widely read books, *The Cost of Discipleship* and *Life Together,* deeply influenced those who later struggled for human rights in South Africa and Latin America. Bonhoeffer brought a new dimension to Christian discipleship by distinguishing between "cheap" and "costly" grace. To him, cheap

> **World changers are willing to lay down their lives for their beliefs.**
>
> •
>
> *They could find no charge or fault, because he was faithful.*
>
> Daniel 6:4 NKJV

grace was embodied by preaching forgiveness, allowing baptism, and giving communion without requiring true repentance, discipline, and confession. He wrote, "The immanent righteousness of history only rewards and punishes the deeds of men, the eternal righteousness of God tries and judges their hearts."[11]

DANIEL BOONE
(1734–1820)

❧

"A Life That Spawned Bigger-Than-Life Legends"

Brave, kind, honest, and simple.

Robbed, cheated, dispossessed.

Both sets of adjectives have been used to describe Daniel Boone, the son of a Quaker blacksmith who became known around the world as the supreme freelance frontiersman and a man "ordained by God to settle the wilderness." In all likelihood, Boone was a man who was a blend of the above descriptors, plus the words *hopeful* and *restless*.

Boone developed an early interest in hunting and exploring while an agent for the Transylvania Company. He was not, as folklore claimed, a man who loved solitude. To the end of his life, he protested openly that he loved having friends and neighbors. Neither was Boone a great Indian slayer, as some accounts of his life have relayed. He once told his son Nathan that he was sure of having killed only one person, a warrior at the battle of Blue Licks.

Stories circulated that Boone was a man of vast muscular strength and gigantic stature. In actuality, he was 5 feet, 8 or 9 inches tall and slender. Writer James Kirke Paulding wrote that Boone could "march to the north pole, and shoot out the wind's eye, if it were no bigger than the point of a needle." In reality, he often aimed and missed.

In most cases, the "bigger-than-life" Daniel Boone was a fictional character. He initially was the subject of author John Filson who wrote an "autobiography" of Boone that was published in 1784. The book was a great success in Europe, more so than in America. Boone liked the book and said simply, "All true . . . every word true." A larger volume was written by an in-law, Daniel Bryan, and was published in 1813—about this book, Boone regretted that "he could not sue him for slander." Lord Byron described Boone in glowing terms, and James Fenimore Cooper characterized him in four of his novels. His reported exploits appeared in Audubon's *Ornithological Biography,* and he became the popular subject of short stories and magazine articles.

The folklore resulted in Boone's having a county in Virginia named for him in 1847, a day named in his honor in Kentucky, and major celebrations held in honor of the 200th anniversary of his birth. He was the subject of a popular portrait painted by George Caleb Bingham, and a series of dime store novels were written about him by Frederick Whittaker. In the 1940s, a comic strip drawn by C. C. Cooper retold the stories of his exploits for the Sunday papers.

The shadow cast by a real world changer is always bigger than life.

•

You will show me the path of life; In Your presence is fullness of joy.

Psalm 16:11 NKJV

What was it that drew fiction writers to Boone?

It was what *really* made Boone a hero: his undying belief that a better life might be found just around the next bend. When he lost his land in Kentucky owing to faulty titles, he moved to Missouri. Again, he lost his land there, only to have it later restored by Congress. As he sought to trailblaze his own life, he helped trailblaze the Wilderness Road.

Consistently, Boone refused to give in to defeats, and he refused to settle for a "second best" life. He continued to move deeper and deeper into the frontier of his nation in search of respect and a decent living.[12]

LOUIS BRAILLE
(1809-1852)

❦

"He Gave A New System Of Reading And Writing To The Blind"

It was frustration that drove Louis to seek innovative solutions—a frustration that began when he was only four years old. While playing with an awl and leather strip in his father's saddle and harness shop, Louis had an accident that left one eye punctured. Infection set in, and before the incident was over, he had lost sight permanently in both eyes.

From the beginning, Louis was determined that he would find his way without a cane or assistance. He slowly but persistently developed the necessary mobility skills to navigate his home, yard, and town. When he was old enough, he attended the village school where he listened intently and tried to memorize every word the schoolmaster spoke. Louis, however, could not read or write, and he was frustrated at falling behind his classmates.

At age ten, Louis was sent to a school for blind children in Paris. Gradually, he became accustomed to his new surroundings and became an eager student of "embossing"—large letters impressed into thick, heavy paper—the best system of reading and writing for the blind at the time. The first sentence he wrote in embossing was, "My name is Louis Braille."

Louis was excited about learning to read and write, but he was frustrated that the process was so slow. He found greater satisfaction in taking organ and piano lessons, and he practiced for hours. Then, Charles Barbier visited Louis's school. Barbier had developed a system called "night-writing." Based on military codes for transmitting secret messages at night, the system was based on a series of raised dots. The dot clusters or symbols, however, were extremely complex and difficult to read. Since they represented sounds rather than letters of the alphabet, the system was a step removed from conventional writing and had no means for punctuation or numbers.

Fascinated by the system, Louis began to experiment with it and to improvise changes. From the age of twelve to fifteen, he worked long hours—sometimes all night and to the detriment of his own health—to completely overhaul the Barbier system. The system he developed was also based on raised dots, but it was simple and complete, could be written and read quickly, and held the promise of being used in many ways beyond books. His fellow students and teachers mastered the system quickly and saw it as a great improvement. His system was applicable to any language, to mathematics, and to longhand or shorthand. Before he was twenty, Louis had even applied his system to musical notation.

The greatest challenge Louis faced was a political one. Significant contracts had been given to embossers. It was to be another twenty years of constant effort and frustration before Braille's system was publicly acknowledged as the new standard. Braille died at age forty-three after years of illness, not knowing that his system would gain worldwide acceptance but knowing in his heart that he had given the greatest gift ever made to the blind. The plaque on the front of his childhood home acknowledges that he "opened the doors of knowledge to all those who cannot see."[13]

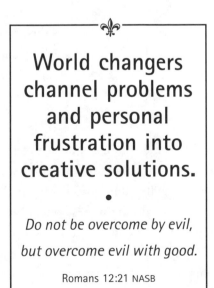

World changers channel problems and personal frustration into creative solutions.

•

Do not be overcome by evil, but overcome evil with good.

Romans 12:21 NASB

MICHELANGELO BUONARROTI
(1475–1564)

"He Gave The World Beauty Beyond Imagination"

The Sistine Chapel of the Vatican had long been a place for prayer and the site of elections for popes. It was Pope Julius II, however, who thought the decoration of the chapel was too dull and who selected Michelangelo Buonarroti for the project of redoing the chapel's ceiling. Michelangelo protested that he was a sculptor, not a painter—the fact actually was that he *preferred* sculpting, and he knew that painting a vaulted ceiling sixty feet in the air was a process that would take years and would require the development of a new painting technique. Pope Julius prevailed, however, and Michelangelo began four years of isolated, back-breaking work on the project that was to become his most famous one.

In the beginning, Michelangelo hired other well-known fresco painters to assist him, but after seeing their first efforts, he dismissed them, pulled down what they had done, and closed himself in the chapel to do the work alone. Much of the experience was miserable for him. Pope Julius alternately nagged him and forgot to pay him. He battled poor health as well as mold and dampness in the chapel, his own clothes even rotting on his body; and he faced the constant battle of painting figures in perspective on a vaulted, curved surface. He wrote that he often felt as if he was wasting his time "without any results." He often *repainted* figures that he had thought were complete. A friend of Michelangelo asked him why he took such pains with figures that would be seen only at a distance. "Who will know whether it is perfect or not?" he asked. Michelangelo responded, "I will."

Michelangelo persevered until, in the end, he completed the largest and most famous fresco in the world. He once wrote, "I strain more than any man who ever lived . . . and with great exhaustion; and yet I have the patience to arrive at the desired goal."

When the chapel frescoes were completed, they covered 5,800 square feet and had more than 300 figures. Theologians praised the themes of his work. Art critics hailed the beauty of his work and commented on the intricacy of the figures. Countless millions of visitors through the centuries have stood in awe at what he portrayed.

His entire life seemed embodied by patient perseverance toward perfection. He spent fourteen years as lead architect and artist for the New Sacristy in Florence that was to house the tombs of Medici family members. He also built the Laurentian Library for the Medicis, which incorporated several architectural innovations. His building projects included the Campidoglio Square civic center and St. Peter's interior.

As a sculptor, Michelangelo's works are among the most famous in the world: the *Pieta* in St. Peter's, *David, Moses,* and the *Dying Slave* and *Rebellious Slave*—

> # World changers persevere in their pursuit of excellence.
>
> •
>
> *Blessed is a man who perseveres under trial; for once he has been approved, he will receive the crown of life.*
>
> James 1:12 NASB

the last two of which were for the tomb of the pope who hired and nagged him to complete the Sistine Chapel, Julius II.

As part of his will, Michelangelo had these words included, "I die in the faith of Jesus Christ, and in the firm hope of a better life."[14]

ANDREW CARNEGIE
(1835-1919)

⚜

"Extreme Generosity To The Public Good"

Andrew Carnegie was born in Scotland and immigrated to the United States at the age of thirteen, where he found work earning a dollar a week as a weaver's assistant in a cotton factory. Few would have predicted he would become one of the wealthiest and most powerful industrialists in the nation.

As a messenger boy in a Pittsburgh telegraph office, Carnegie learned telegraphy. He advanced quickly to become a division superintendent for the Pennsylvania Railroad. Through friendship with the inventor of the "sleeping car," he became a part of the Woodruff Sleeping Car Company and made his first small fortune. He invested some of his earnings in Pennsylvania oil lands and increased his wealth enormously. After the Civil War, he entered the iron business. In 1868, he introduced the Bessemer process into the steel industry and established steel works in Pennsylvania and elsewhere. Carnegie consolidated all of his interests in 1899 into the Carnegie Steel Company, and two years later he retired from business with a fortune estimated at a half-billion dollars.

Carnegie then turned to philanthropy as his "occupation." In 1912, he announced the creation of a foundation that he had funded with $125 million to carry out his philanthropic schemes, which already exceeded $200 million. He desired to die a poor man, but at his death, he was still worth some $22 million.

Having been a factory worker himself, he was very concerned about the personal welfare of workers and established a multimillion-dollar benefit fund for the employees of the Carnegie Steel Company. He also gave millions to various peace-related enterprises. As a writer, he vigorously denounced war, and his books *The Gospel of Wealth, The Empire of Business,* and *Problems of Today* became international bestsellers.

With very little formal education himself, Carnegie gave generously to educational institutions. He was a major benefactor of the Carnegie Institute of Technology in Pittsburgh, and he gave generously to Saint Andrews and Aberdeen universities in Scotland. A gift of $15 million to the Carnegie Foundation for the Advancement of Teaching was designated to aid teachers in their retirement. Carnegie Hero Funds provided financial gifts to help widows, orphans, and those who were incapacitated for heroic attempts to save human life. The Carnegie Institute, which he funded initially with a gift of $22 million, was established to encourage research into ways to improve the general welfare of mankind. More than $50 million was given to help libraries.

A reporter once asked Carnegie the secret of his success. He replied, "I owe it all to my flashes. . . . I woke up early in the morning and always there came into my mind

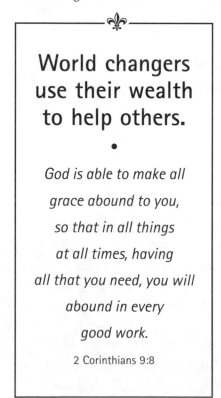

World changers use their wealth to help others.

•

God is able to make all grace abound to you, so that in all things at all times, having all that you need, you will abound in every good work.

2 Corinthians 9:8

with the waking a flash telling me what to do that day, and if I followed those flashes, I always succeeded."

The reporter then asked, "You mean that you have heavenly visions, and like the man in the Scriptures you were not disobedient to your visions?"

With a smile Carnegie replied, "Call it that if you like . . . it was the following of those silent admonitions and directions which brought me the success you say I have achieved."[15]

JIMMY CARTER
(1924)

❧

"Champion Of Human Rights"

James Earl Carter Jr. was born into a close-knit family in an isolated rural community. Home was his haven, and most of his impressions of the world were gained from a battery radio. Then, at age eighteen, he entered the United States Naval Academy, and the world began to become his home.

After his Navy term of duty, Carter was selected by Admiral Rickover to work on the atomic submarine project. The next year, however, his father died, and Carter returned to Plains, Georgia, to manage the family business. He was elected as a state legislator in 1962. A failed bid for the governorship in 1966 left him deeply depressed, which led him on a spiritual search that resulted in a deeply profound conversion experience. With renewed devotion to Christ Jesus, he was baptized and dedicated his life to following Jesus' teachings. He worked for a time as a Baptist lay preacher and then returned to politics; he was elected as governor of Georgia in 1970. He reorganized the state government to reduce the number of agencies and to create a budget surplus; he also enacted several environmental measures and overhauled the state's social services bureaucracy. On the foundation of these successes, he announced his candidacy for president in 1974, and he was elected President of the United States in 1976.

President Carter saw the Panama Canal treaties ratified by the Senate, energy bills passed by Congress, and diplomatic relations normalized with China. He also witnessed the signing of the Camp David Accords between Israel and Egypt. He was a strong advocate for human rights, and he took deep satisfaction that what Jefferson had said about his presidency was also true for his term: "Not a drop of the blood of a single citizen was shed by the sword of war."

In his own words, Carter said about his failed bid for re-election, "Rosalynn and I were devastated." At age fifty-six, Carter felt he was too young to retire. He returned to Plains to discover the family business a million dollars in debt, and he set himself to restoring it. He spent a great deal of time in self-analysis and prayer. "Putting the problem in God's hands gives me a degree of peace that lets me live with the outcome, whatever it may be."

As a "distinguished professor" at Emory University, Carter found renewed purpose. He also wrote his memoirs, built The Carter Center to address international problems, and began doing active volunteer work with Habitat for Humanity, building homes for "God's people in need." Through The Carter Center he has supervised projects to eradicate disease and introduce new crop hybrids in Africa, immunize Third World children, promote human rights through free elections, and promote peace among those engaged in civil wars. In the years since his presidency, his work has been almost entirely among the poorest and most needy people in the United States and foreign nations. Statesman Henry Kissinger said of him, "He is simply dedicated to serving his country . . . a true missionary of peace."[16]

> # World changers champion human rights for all people.
>
> •
>
> *When Christ returns how glad I will be that my work among you was so worthwhile.*
>
> Philippians 2:16 TLB

GEORGE WASHINGTON CARVER

(1864–1943)

⚜

"He Changed The Agriculture Of The South"

George Washington Carver was born during the Civil War in Missouri, and since his mother was a slave of Moses Carver, he was known in his early years simply as "Carver's George." Moses Carver was a hard-working farmer who did not approve of slavery but had no other way of acquiring farm hands. The Carvers raised George as they would have raised a son, giving him a few chores to do and allowing him to explore the woods after his chores were finished. He became fascinated with the natural world.

With their blessing, George left the Carvers to search for a Negro school when he was just a boy. He earned a living as a cook, house-worker, laundryman, and seamster. It was as he enrolled at school that he adopted the name "George Washington Carver." When he felt he was ready, he applied to colleges and was eventually accepted at Simpson College in Iowa. Then in 1894, he transferred from there to Iowa State College. Upon graduation, he was offered a faculty post teaching systematic botany.

In 1896, the administrators at Tuskegee Institute in Alabama offered Professor Carver the opportunity to head its newly formed department of agriculture, and he jumped at the opportunity, even though the department was largely "on paper only." Carver put together a laboratory and began the work that would become his life. He began a campaign of education for every farmer he met. He taught farmers to rotate their crops and virtually single-handedly launched and promoted the peanut industry as an alternative to cotton. He identified one hundred and forty-five useful products made from peanuts and lobbied hard for a tariff on peanuts so the peanut industry might develop.

He also developed a number of medicines from barks and herbs, discovered unusual dyes and pigments, and found countless new uses for old products—and he never took out a patent or sought to commercialize his findings. He was interested only in helping other human beings. Above all, he valued a simple life of research and teaching. He received numerous awards and honors in agricultural chemistry, both in the United States and England, and in later years, he poured his life's savings into the Carver Foundation for agricultural research. He and President Franklin Delano Roosevelt spoke often of their joint desire to see people everywhere "better fed, better housed, and better clothed."

Also an artist, Carver never thought it unusual that he enjoyed embroidery, knitting, crochet, and painting. He enjoyed designing unusual patterns and working with different textures. Painting, and creating and collecting delicate handicrafts were his lifelong hobbies.

Carver was never ashamed of his faith. When a reporter once asked him about his philosophy of life, he

> **World changers are never linked to race, creed, or color—only character.**
>
> •
>
> *Seek first His kingdom and His righteousness; and all these things shall be added to you.*
>
> Matthew 6:33 NASB

replied, "I go into the woods, and there I gather specimens and study the great lessons that Nature is eager to teach us. Alone in the woods each morning I best hear and understand God's plan for me."[17]

WINSTON CHURCHILL
(1874-1965)

⚜

"He Personified Resistance to Tyranny"

Sir Winston Churchill held most of the high offices of state in Great Britain. He was a member of Parliament for more than sixty years and twice served as prime minister. He was Britain's leader through most of World War II.

From his childhood, he loved to read history and poetry and had an outstanding memory. Churchill was the third son of the seventh Duke of Marlborough; his mother was an American. He rejected the idea of attending a university, however, and enrolled in the Royal Military College at Sandhurst. He served in Cuba and India and took part in the Battle of Omdurman in the Sudan (1898). While in the military, he wrote for British newspapers. Later the *Morning Post* sent him to cover the South African War, and his capture and daring escape from the Boers made him an overnight celebrity.

Elected to Parliament as a Conservative in 1900, Churchill at first found speaking an ordeal. In 1904, he changed his political affiliation to become a Liberal. He worked closely with Admiral Lord Fisher of Kilverstone to prepare the British navy for World War I and himself served a period of active service in France. In the 1920s, he again aligned himself with the Conservatives, noting that "any fool can rat, but I flatter myself that it takes a certain ingenuity to re-rat." He did not hold office between 1929 and 1939, but he voiced strong opposition to England's

"Indian policy" and warned repeatedly against the ambitions of Nazi Germany. He became prime minister on May 10, 1940, and he served until 1945. He was largely responsible for many aspects of England's war policy. He again served as prime minister from 1951 to 1955.

In addition to his political contributions, he remained a noted historian, producing the four-volume *History of the English-Speaking Peoples,* four-volume *The World Crisis,* four-volume *Marlborough,* and six-volume *The Second World War.*

Churchill is perhaps best remembered for his radio addresses that rallied his nation and instilled courage in his fellow citizens when German invasion seemed likely. He pledged his "blood, toil, tears, and sweat" to the defeat of Germany. Undoubtedly his most famous statement was this:

"We shall go to the end, we shall fight in France, we shall fight on the seas and oceans, we shall fight with growing confidence and growing strength in the air, we shall defend our Island whatever the cost may be, we shall fight on the landing grounds, we shall fight in the fields and in the streets, we shall fight in the hills; we shall never surrender, and even if, which I do not for a moment believe, this Island or a large part of it were subjugated and starving, then our Empire beyond the seas, armed and guarded by the British Fleet, would carry on the struggle, until, in God's good time, the New World, with all its power and might steps forth to the rescue and the liberation of the old."[18]

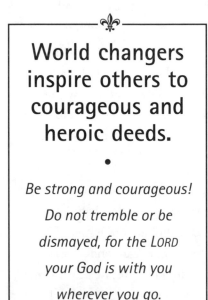

World changers inspire others to courageous and heroic deeds.

•

Be strong and courageous! Do not tremble or be dismayed, for the LORD your God is with you wherever you go.

Joshua 1:9 NASB

CHUCK COLSON
(1931)

❧

"He Turned Personal Error and Tragedy into Help for a Forgotten Population"

Chuck Colson's father told him two things when Chuck was a child: "First, always tell the truth. And second, whatever you put your mind to—it doesn't matter if it's cleaning toilets—do it with excellence." Colson added to this character—building from this advice the words of the Marine motto: *Semper Fidelis* (always faithful), and on that three-pronged platform, he completed his studies at a prestigious college, served in the Marines, and then embarked on a "fast-track" career to the top. By age twenty-four he was assistant to the Assistant Secretary of the Navy, then served as administrative assistant to a United States Senator (while he completed law school), and finally, was the senior partner of a law firm in Washington, D.C. In 1969, he answered a call he had been anticipating all his life: the president of the United States needed him.

As Special Counsel to President Richard Nixon, Colson moved in a circle of power. He gained a reputation as a man who could get a job done. Personally, Colson began to regard public office not only as a trust and duty, but also as a "holy crusade." He justified actions he previously would have questioned in his political zeal to preserve personal power. Colson left the White House in 1973 to establish the law firm Colson and Shapiro. Shortly thereafter a client bluntly told him about Jesus Christ and read to him a passage from C. S. Lewis's *Mere*

Christianity. The message struck home, and in his client's driveway, Colson found himself praying over and over to God, "Take me." His conversion became front-page news and was ridiculed by his former political foes. Supported by new Christian friends, however, he found the strength to plead guilty to a Watergate offense for which he had not even been charged: passing derogatory information to the press regarding an anti-war activist.

In Maxwell Federal Prison, Colson served seven months as prisoner #23226. When not working at the prison's washing machine, he studied the Bible, met with fellow Christians, and began to grapple with understanding why prisoners were not rehabilitated. After his release from prison, he wrote his widely circulated autobiography, *Born Again.* With the royalties and the help of Christian friends, he founded Prison Fellowship in 1976 to introduce prisoners to Christ, disciple them, and equip them for life "on the outside." Within fifteen years, Prison Fellowship grew to a network of 40,000 Christian workers in the United States and thousands more overseas. Through this organization, outreaches have been made to inmates' families, gifts have been given to prisoners' children, a restoration program has been established for victims of crime, and a restitution program to communities has been initiated through inmate work projects.

> ❧
>
> # World changers often do their work with passion and urgency born of personal experience.
>
> •
>
> *I was hungry and you fed me; I was thirsty and you gave me water; I was a stranger and you invited me into your homes; Naked and you clothed me; sick and in prison, and you visited me.*
>
> Matthew 25:35–36 TLB

Colson sees his broader work as challenging Christians everywhere to put their faith into *action*. His own efforts have included an extensive writing and speaking schedule. He is known as a man with "urgency" written into his facial expressions. He has written, "We are not just engaged in some vague philanthropic exercise. We are dealing with life and death. And we had better get on with this business of proclaiming the Gospel!"[19]

CHRISTOPHER COLUMBUS
(1451–1506)

❧

"He Opened Up A New World"

Although some argue as to whether Christopher Columbus was the first European to "discover" America, few debate his role as the first to open up a way for exploring and settling a "new world."

In his lifetime, however, Columbus was not regarded as a hero. He was scorned and ridiculed during his long years of preparation as a half-insane fanatic, and he was often neglected or abused after his voyages. In actuality, he was a clear-thinking man of great faith, who faced an opposition that would have left a less-committed person completely overwhelmed.

"Christoforo Colombo" was an Italian who grew up with a love for the sea. He went to sea as a teenager and made possible voyages to England and Iceland. He became an excellent mapmaker in the process. It was after marrying a woman in Lisbon that he came into possession of her family's navigational charts. Those charts, along with his own experience and his reading of the adventures of Marco Polo, made him determined to find a direct route to the East.

The idea of a "round" earth was proposed by Aristotle, but even in Columbus's time, few believed it. Columbus was willing to risk his life to find out. He began immediately to seek funding for a voyage. After being turned down in Genoa and Portugal, he went to Spain and spent years presenting his case to Isabella and Ferdinand. From time to time, he retreated to monasteries to rest, and while at a convent at La Rahiba, he met Juan Perez, Queen Isabella's former confessor. Perez wrote a letter to the queen on Columbus's behalf, and the queen subsequently sold some of her personal jewels to outfit three vessels for the voyage, the largest of which was only 163 feet long.

On August 3, 1492, Columbus set sail from Palos—sailing straight into the "Sea of Darkness." They sailed for weeks without any sign of land. Even when the crew threatened mutiny, Columbus remained firm and refused to turn back. Signs of land eventually appeared, and early in the morning on October 12, the ships landed. Columbus named the landing site San Salvador (now a Bahamian island). In December he landed at "Espanola" (now Haiti).

Columbus made three more voyages to the Western Hemisphere. During the third voyage he was greatly discouraged to find his "colonies" in disarray and tried in vain to restore order. A governor sent from Spain placed him in chains and had him sent back to Spain. In 1502, he made his fourth voyage but again encountered difficulties as well as personal illness. He died in disappointment in 1506, never knowing the lands he had discovered were *not* Japan.

Throughout his life, Columbus had a strong sense of spiritual vision regarding his voyages. His first act upon landing at San Salvador was to plant a cross and to commission his sailors to preach the Gospel to those they might

> # The full accomplishment of genuine world changers may not be recognized until long after their death.
>
> •
>
> *Commit to the Lord whatever you do, and your plans will succeed*
>
> Proverbs 16:3

encounter. He spoke often of being under the illumination of the Holy Spirit. In 1502, he wrote to Ferdinand and Isabella: "In the carrying out of this enterprise of the Indies, neither reason nor mathematics nor maps were any use to me: fully accomplished were the words of Isaiah" (regarding the gathering of a remnant of Israel in the last days).[20]

Jacques-Yves Cousteau
(1910–1997)

❧

"He Opened Up the World Under the Seas"

Jacques Cousteau once said, "When I was four or five years old, I loved touching water. Water fascinated me—first floating ships, then me floating and stones not floating." Cousteau developed two other great loves in his life: gadgets and filmmaking. He spent his life combining his three passions.

His father was an international business manager, and the family traveled a great deal. Cousteau was born in a village near Bordeaux, France. The young Cousteau made his first underwater dive at a summer camp in Vermont when he was ten years old, helping clear a lake of dead twigs and branches.

At age eleven, he built a model of a machine for loading cargo onto ships. Two years later, he wrote and published on a mimeograph machine his own book, *An Adventure in Mexico*. Next, he bought a secondhand movie camera and printed stationery: "FILMS ZIX—Jack Cousteau producer, director, and chief camera man." His father confiscated the stationery, however, until his schoolwork improved!

At age nineteen, Cousteau entered the French naval academy because, in his words, "I thought it was a good way to go places." Four years later, he was a naval officer. Then, tragedy struck. He was seriously injured in an automobile accident and for months, could not move either arm. Much of his effort to regain the use and strength of his arms involved swimming in the sea. His first underwater dive with goggles gave his life a new direction.

In 1937, he married Simone Melchior, who also had a great love for the sea, and they, along with their two sons, began a lifetime pursuit of experiments and the invention of devices to make underwater exploration easier. Cousteau and French engineer Emile Gagnan developed a Self-Contained Underwater Breathing Apparatus—scuba for short—that was patented under the name "Aqua-Lung." The world that Cousteau discovered on his Aqua-Lung dives was one he wanted to share. He developed a watertight case for his old movie camera and began to take the world's first underwater pictures. During World War II, the French military assigned him to full-time underwater research, which included locating and dismantling underwater mines, finding shipwrecks, and filming torpedoes launched from submarines. Two of his films won prizes at the new Cannes Film Festival.

> **World changers turn their passions into exploration, and their explorations into passions to help others.**
>
> •
>
> *The LORD is the great God, the great King above all gods. . . . The sea is his, for he made it, and his hands formed the dry land.*
>
> Psalms 95:3-5

In 1950, Cousteau began a new chapter in ocean research with the outfitting of a ship he named *Calypso*. His motto became, "We must go and see for ourselves." In *Calypso,* he and his crew of scientists traveled from the Amazon to the Red Sea, Alaska to Antarctica. The French government, along with family and friends financed his early expeditions. His wife even sold her jewelry to help pay the bills. Later, earnings from books, films, and American television networks, provided the funding he needed. In all, he wrote more than fifty books and made more than sixty television documentaries about life under the sea. In 1973, he formed the Cousteau Society to help combat the pollution of the world's oceans and water ways.[21]

WALTER CRONKITE

(1916)

❧

"His Name Became Synonymous with Trustworthiness"

Walter Cronkite grew up in Kansas City as an all-American kid, playing sports, fishing, swimming, and flying kites. Although he was an only child, he had lots of friends and a large extended family. He worked in his grandfather's pharmacy and was influenced by the kindness his grandfather showed to the poor who could not pay for their medications. His family moved to Houston, and it was there, at San Jacinto High School, that Walter had a chance to begin a career as a journalist. He worked as a reporter for the school paper and wrote for the school yearbook.

At the University of Texas Cronkite took courses in journalism and wrote campus news for the *Houston Post*. He also was a sportscaster for a Houston radio station and wrote political stories for the Scripps-Howard chain. He dropped out of college to become a full-time reporter for the *Houston Post*. He later worked for KCMO in Kansas City as a sportscaster and as a writer for United Press. He was a war correspondent for UP in Europe, and after the war, he set up UP news bureaus in Belgium, Holland, and Luxembourg. He eventually returned to radio reporting, this time in Washington, D.C.

In 1950, Cronkite became one of the first journalists to work for a TV network, CBS. He reported daily on the Korean War for the network and then covered the presidential conventions in 1952. His live reports made him nationally famous. He began to travel around the world covering major stories. His weekly programs, *You Are There* and the *Sunday News Special,* were highly popular.

At CBS, Cronkite was assigned to cover all space coverage, beginning in 1956. He later said he enjoyed that assignment more than any other. He became an expert on space and reported all of the major space events, including Alan Shepard's first ride into space, John Glenn's orbit of the earth, and Neil Armstrong's first steps on the moon. In 1962, Cronkite took over the job of anchoring the *CBS Evening News.* His coverage of John F. Kennedy's assassination was the only time he cried during a newscast. Later, he covered the assassinations of Robert Kennedy and Martin Luther King Jr. Cronkite ended each of his *CBS Evening News* shows with the words, "And that's the way it is." For millions of Americans, his words were irrefutable truth. The only opinion Cronkite ever voiced on a broadcast was this statement urging peace with the Vietnamese: "We lived up to our pledge to defend democracy, and we did the best we could." He was a strong advocate for the freedom of the press and defended his views in many speeches and in an appearance before Congress. He became instrumental in bringing Anwar Sadat of Egypt and Menachim Begin of Israel together for a peace accord that culminated in an agreement at Camp David.

During his more than forty years in the news business, Cronkite covered many of the world's major stories, criss-crossing the globe many times. Public opinion polls consistently show him to be the most trusted person in America, and his news shows are considered the standard by which all other TV news shows are measured.[22]

> # World changers are people of excellent reputation.
>
> •
>
> *A GOOD name is rather to be chosen than great riches, and loving favour rather than silver and gold.*
>
> Proverbs 22:1 KJV

FANNY CROSBY
(1820–1915)

❧

"She Gave the World Some of Its Favorite Hymns"

When Fanny Jane Crosby was only six weeks old, she lost her sight as the result of a doctor's error in treating an illness. She never voiced bitterness about her blindness, however, and once stated, "I have always believed that the good Lord, in His infinite mercy, by this means consecrated me to the work that I am still permitted to do." When a Scottish minister tried to express sorrow at her blindness, she quickly replied, "If I had been given a choice at birth, I would have asked to be blind . . . for when I get to Heaven, the first face I will see will be the one who died for me."

At age fifteen, she entered the New York Institute for the Blind, where she received an excellent education. She later taught there, and at the age of thirty-eight, she married Alexander van Alstyne, who was also blind. He was an organist in two New York City churches, and his musical knowledge helped her in countless ways. They were married for forty-four years.

Although Crosby did not begin her life's work of writing hymns until she was forty years old, she ultimately wrote the text for more than 8,000 hymns, using more than 200 pen names. Under contract to a music publisher, she wrote 3 new hymns each week during much of her life. From 1865 to 1905, she produced nearly 200 songs a year. Her hymns have been noted by generations for their thoughtful and praise-filled texts. Her work has been translated into numerous foreign languages and distributed by the millions in English-speaking areas.

Many of Crosby's songs were written in collaboration with her friend William H. Doane. At times, Crosby would write the lyrics first; at other times Doane would write a song, and Crosby would respond, "That tune says to me . . ." and write a stirring text. Phoebe Palmer Knapp, wife of the founder of Metropolitan Life Insurance Company, composed a tune in 1873, and she brought it to Crosby in Brooklyn. Crosby asked Knapp to play the tune for her on the organ as Crosby knelt in prayer nearby. She played it a second time and then a third. The blind woman finally responded, "That says, 'Blessed assurance, Jesus is mine! O what a foretaste of glory divine!'" The hymn "Blessed Assurance" is one of her most famous.

Among her best-known hymns are, "Jesus, Keep Me Near the Cross," "Draw Me Nearer," "Rescue the Perishing," "I Am Thine, O Lord," and "All the Way My Saviour Leads Me." Her song "To God Be the Glory" was popular in both D. L. Moody's evangelistic campaigns in England and also in the Billy Graham crusades across America.

In addition to her work as a musical poetess, Crosby loved to visit the rescue missions in New York City. There she would make what she called a "pressing plea" for any boy present who had "wandered from his mother's home and teaching" to see her at the end of the service. She had numerous opportunities to share her faith in Christ with those who responded to her plea.[23]

> # World changers focus on possibilities, not on limitations.
>
> •
>
> *Oh, sing to the LORD a new song! For He has done marvelous things.*
>
> Psalm 98:1 NKJV

MARIE CURIE

(1867–1934)

"Undeterred By Hardship or Sorrow"

Little Marie had no idea why her beautiful and loving mother never kissed her. It was only after her mother died when Marie was eleven that she learned her mother had tuberculosis. Her mother's death only compounded the sorrow Marie had felt at the death of her older sister. Their deaths were the first of many hardships and sorrows she would face in her life.

At age nineteen, Marie left her poverty-stricken home to take a position as a governess. For three years, she taught in an environment that left her feeling lonely and unhappy. She sent every extra penny she earned to help her brother get an education. When her brother finished his schooling, Marie saved her money to buy a one-way fourth-class ticket to Paris. There, she began her own university studies. She found that her scientific studies, especially, were more exciting than any fairy tale she had ever read.

As a student, Marie lived as simply and cheaply as possible, traveling to the university on foot in all kinds of weather and spending her evenings at the library so she didn't have to heat her small rented room. She continued this way through a master's degree and then two more degrees—one in physics, one in mathematics. She did not seem to mind her poverty. She was enthralled with her studies and her friends, one of whom was Pierre Curie, a fellow scientist devoted to research. They were married without fanfare. In fact, when a friend insisted on buying her wedding dress, Marie said, "If you are going to be kind enough to give me one, please let it be practical and dark, so that I can put it on afterward to go into the laboratory."

Marie was relentless in her determination to isolate radium, scorning fatigue and financial problems, not to mention a damp, icy-cold shed that was the Curies' laboratory. She often forgot to eat or sleep. In the end, they succeeded—she and Pierre won the Nobel Prize in 1903 for their discovery of radium. No woman had ever achieved such acclaim in science. The Curies might have profited greatly from their research and fame, but they decided neither to take out patents nor to profit materially from their discovery.

Only three years later, Pierre was killed in a street accident in Paris. At age thirty-eight, Marie entered a new realm of loneliness and sadness. She continued her work, however, without giving in to her anguish. In 1911, she was awarded the Nobel Prize in chemistry, becoming the first person to receive the Nobel Prize twice.

When World War I began, Marie gave all she had to assist France. She installed her X-ray apparatus wherever it was most needed and helped surgeons in their operations. She is estimated to have installed more than 200 radiological rooms, which were used to help more than a million soldiers.

> ⚜
>
> # World changers often give up personal comfort in their quest for discoveries that will help others.
>
> •
>
> *[Wisdom]: Take my instructions, and not silver, And knowledge rather than choicest gold. For wisdom is better than jewels; And all desirable things can not compare to her.*
>
> Proverbs 8:10–11 NASB

In her later years, Madame Curie suffered ill health and experienced degenerating eyesight. A professor noted, "Madame Curie can be counted among the eventual victims of the radioactive bodies which she and her husband discovered." Nonetheless, her discovery of radiation led to treatments that have saved the lives of millions through the years.[24]

LEONARDO DA VINCI
(1452-1519)

⚜

"A Genius Ahead of His Time"

Many consider Leonardo da Vinci to be the greatest genius in history. He embodied an entire era—the Italian Renaissance—as an artist, scientist, engineer, architect, inventor, and musician. His ideas were often scorned, however, by those who knew him because they were so far ahead of their time.

Leonardo was recognized as a genius from his childhood and was apprenticed to a leading artist in Florence to study painting, sculpture, music, science, and mathematics. While still a young man, he moved to Milan and worked there for the city's "ruler" as an artist, musician, engineer, inventor, and producer of parades and pageants. For him, there was no line between art and science. His notebooks were filled with ideas and illustrations that showed plants and animals in realistic detail. He studied the flight of birds and observed patterns of water and wind, light and shadow, and the movement of stars. He drew sketches of airplanes, armored tanks, paddleboats, and many other mechanical devices that were not "invented" until modern times. He was a mapmaker, bridge designer, and medical theorist (predicting a prime cause for the spread of epidemics). To keep his notes private, he wrote backwards: to read his ideas, a person had to hold his notes in front of a mirror.

As diligent as he was in science and math, he also placed great value upon reflection. He often sat for days without moving as he waited for inspiration for a new idea or image to fill his mind. For days he waited for the moment when he felt the face of Christ was revealed to him for his painting of the *Last Supper*—when the image came to him, he painted it quickly and with an air of certainty.

In spite of his great imagination and skill, many of his projects were never completed. Others were lost or damaged. The *Last Supper* began to disintegrate shortly after its completion because of a new paint formula he had tried. When Milan was invaded by France in 1499, he went from one Italian city-state to another, never able to settle down and concentrate on any one project for very long. While he was often commissioned to design weapons and defense systems, he found war "a bestial madness."

As an old man, he worked for King Francis I in France. He filled thousands of pages with ideas, hoping they would be published after his death to help humanity. Instead, they were hidden in collections across Europe for nearly 300 years. Most of his paintings were lost, but those that survived have been highly praised. His portrait *Mona Lisa* is perhaps the most famous painting in history.

As a young man, Leonardo da Vinci was popular—strong, handsome, witty, a practical joker, and a sought-out conversationalist. As he grew older and became more accomplished, people stated that while they admired him, they did

---

World changers sometimes suffer from the neglect or misunderstanding of their peers.

•

I have directed you in the way of wisdom; I have led you in upright paths. When you walk, your steps will not be impeded; And if you run you will not stumble.

Proverbs 4:11-12 NASB

not understand him. While other Renaissance philosophers believed the earth was for people's use, Leonardo saw humans as just small players on a huge stage of existence. He became increasingly isolated. It was only many years after his death that his ideas regained popularity.[25]

CHARLES DICKENS
(1812–1870)

⚜

"He Changed His Society through Fiction"

Considered to be the founder of the modern novel and one of the greatest novelists of all time, Charles Dickens is a man who rose above a sordid and unhappy childhood. Born into a fairly well-to-do family in England, he had what he called a "prodigal father" who became so deeply in debt that he was sent to a debtors' prison. Charles was put to work in a blacking warehouse as a boy, an environment in which he worked hard, received little food, and slept "under the counter like a homeless cat." He became determined that this would not be his life forever.

Dickens managed to go to school for two years, after which he entered a lawyer's office. Although he was little more than an errand boy, he did have time to study, and he also came into contact with people who saw that he had talent. He studied shorthand in his spare time, and at nineteen, he became a newspaper reporter in the House of Commons. A short while later, he began to contribute to various magazines his vivid impressions of London life known as *Sketches by Boz.* These were so popular that publishers bargained for the series, and in 1836, *Pickwick Papers* began to appear as a monthly series.

Several literary innovations are credited to Dickens. With *Oliver Twist,* he introduced the satire of institutions, exposing the abuses of the workhouse system. In *Nicholas Nickleby,* he exposed the management of cheap boarding schools; in *Little Dorrit,* he addressed the evils of the debtors' prison system. Dickens also changed the nature of characters in fiction. He brought to life countless characters who were "as real as the people who walk the streets"—as opposed to the heroic characters of literature in the past. He was one of the first popular authors to grasp the "humor in the absurd" and to champion the causes of the lower class. Perhaps no better illustration of fictional sacrificial love can be found than that of Sidney Carton dying for Charles Darney in Dickens's *Tale of Two Cities.* In the process, Dickens directly contributed to a number of social and industrial reforms.

Although Dickens never taught school, developed a curriculum, or wrote a book directly about education, he is credited with being the greatest educational reformer England has ever produced. By exposing specific abuses in England's educational system, he brought about numerous reforms so that one educator wrote, "not one blow in a thousand is given to a child as compared with the time of Dickens' childhood." The unwholesome restraint of children, the systematic ignoring of children's individuality, and an unsympathetic attitude toward children's creativity were all addressed by Dickens in a way that resulted in reforms.

When asked the secret of his success, Dickens said, "Whatever I have tried to do in life, I have tried with all my heart to do well: Whatever I have devoted myself to, I have devoted myself to completely." In many ways, his own life and the characters of his novels embodied his belief: "No one is useless in this world who lightens the burden of anyone else."[26]

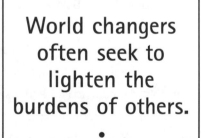

World changers often seek to lighten the burdens of others.

•

Carry each other's burdens, and in this way you will fulfill the law of Christ.

Galatians 6:2

DOROTHEA DIX
(1802–1887)

❧

"A Pioneer in Mental Health Care"

Dorothea Dix grew up in poverty and neglect in a frontier settlement in northern Massachusetts, and at age twelve, she ran away from home to live with her grandmother. Two years later, she went to live with her great-aunt in Worcester. It was the first happy home she knew.

Although she was only fourteen, she opened her own school and taught basic reading and writing skills, social customs, and religion to some twenty students. Three years later she again went to live with her grandmother in Boston. She was influenced by the preaching of William Ellery Channing and came to believe in a loving God who would provide a place of shelter and safety for her. A few years later she opened another school; this time in her grandmother's home—Dix Mansion. Called The Hope, the school was for poor children whom she sought to "rescue . . . from vice and guilt." She wrote a number of books to help her students, including an encyclopedia, *Conversations on Common Things,* which covered 300 topics.

A major illness resulted from Dorothea's heavy work schedule when she was thirty-four. She closed her school and took a trip to Europe for rest; she arrived in Liverpool too ill to travel farther. There, as a guest in the home of the Rathbones, she first learned about the terrible conditions experienced by most of those who were institutionalized as mentally ill.

Dix returned to the United States, and in 1841, she accepted a request to teach Sunday school to women prisoners at the East Cambridge jail. She was appalled at the conditions she found—hungry, cold, insane women huddled in damp, dirty cells. She immediately wrote letters to influential men in Boston asking them to investigate. Action was taken, but Dix began to wonder if other states had been as negligent in caring for the mentally ill. She embarked on a fact-finding mission throughout Massachusetts and found the mentally ill "confined in cages, closets, cellars, stalls, pens . . . chained, naked, beaten with rods, and lashed into obedience" . . . in "filth, neglect, and misery." She wrote a thirty-page "memorial" of her trip and sent it to the state's legislators. A bill was passed that led to an improvement in conditions for the mentally ill.

Her effort had only begun. By 1849, Dix had traveled more than 60,000 miles, visited more than 400 towns, and observed directly more than 9,000 mentally ill people. She not only documented conditions, but also requested funds and legislation. In thirty-five years of this crusade, she had a direct hand in creating thirty-two state hospitals for the mentally ill and a hundred other asylums. Dix, who never married, called the asylums her "children."

Over time, she expanded her concern to the nation's prisons, the poverty of soldiers and sailors, and the care of disabled children. When the Civil War broke out, she was made Superintendent of United States Army Nurses, the highest post in the nation held by a woman. At the time of her death, she was acclaimed as the "most useful and distinguished woman America has produced."[27]

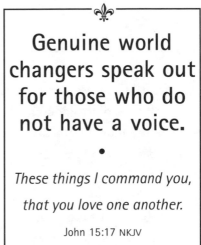

Genuine world changers speak out for those who do not have a voice.

•

These things I command you, that you love one another.

John 15:17 NKJV

FREDERICK DOUGLASS
(1817–1895)

⚜

"A One-Man Force Against Slavery"

There were many things that Frederick Douglass *didn't* know. He was born into slavery in Tuckahoe, Maryland, but like many slaves, he had no knowledge of the year he was born—others estimated it at 1817. His father likely was his white owner, but that also was never confirmed to him. His mother was traded to another plantation shortly after his birth, and he saw her only a few times in secret evening meetings, never really "knowing" her. One thing he *did* know from an early age was that he was determined that he would not be a slave his entire life.

As soon as he was old enough to work, Frederick was put into positions as a house servant and field hand. At age ten, he was assigned by his owner to work as a carpenter's apprentice at a Baltimore shipyard. At twelve, he was leased to a relative of his master, and for a while, the white mistress of that household taught him to read. Frederick later wrote, "The more I learned, the more determined I was to be free." He carried books with him whenever he was sent on an errand and traded scraps of bread for reading lessons from white boys. When his master's son left school, Frederick secretly copied the handwriting in the son's practice book. He once wrote that he "learned to read and write in the only way possible for a slave: I stole the knowledge."

At sixteen, Frederick was leased out again; this time to a very hard taskmaster. He suffered beatings nearly every week of the first six months. Then one day when the slave master came at him with a rope, Frederick resisted. He tossed the man to the ground and fought him, an act unheard of in the slave community. He was never beaten again by the man although he remained a slave for four more years.

In 1838, at the age of twenty-one, Frederick finally succeeded in escaping slavery after his first attempt failed. He made his way to Massachusetts; settled in Bedford with his wife, who was already free; and for several years worked as a day laborer. Then, his story caught the attention of the Massachusetts Anti-Slavery Society, which sent him out to speak across the state. His life in slavery was documented in his book, *Narrative of the Life of Frederick Douglass,* which made him internationally famous. He vowed publicly that "until I die, I will strive for the abolition of slavery and the freedom of all my brethren."

Frederick gave speeches in England to earn enough money to purchase the rights to his own freedom from his owner and also to start an antislavery newspaper called *North Star.* He organized two African-American regiments for the Union Army in the Civil War and after the war, started a second newspaper called *The New National Era.* He became active in state and national politics, and he served as the United States ambassador to Haiti from 1889 to 1891. He published numerous appeals for full civil rights to be given to blacks and also campaigned for the right of women to vote.[28]

> ❧
>
> # World changers have a strong understanding of right and wrong, and they fight for what is right in both word and deed.
>
> •
>
> *Be doers of the word, and not hearers only.*
>
> James 1:22 NKJV

AMELIA EARHART
(1897–1937)

✣

"She Combined Adventure and Service"

Even as a girl, Amelia Earhart had two great desires—a desire for independence and adventure and a desire to help others. As she grew to adulthood, she longed for a career that fulfilled both desires.

During World War I, Amelia visited Canada; and after seeing wounded soldiers, she volunteered as a nurses' aide in a veterans' hospital. She worked ten hours a day at this job until the war ended. Back in the United States, she began to take flying lessons, which was rare for a woman. Even more rare, she bought her own plane! By day, she worked as a professional social worker, and whenever possible, she flew.

In 1927, after Charles Lindbergh made the first solo flight across the Atlantic, a wealthy woman sponsored Amelia to be the first woman to make the same dangerous fight. She crossed the Atlantic in 1928 as the captain of a crew. She wrote a book about the trip, which not only made her famous, but also caught the attention of her publisher, George Putnam. George and Amelia married in 1931, and he supported her flying adventures and published books about them.

Amelia, who was nicknamed A. E., desired to fly the Atlantic by herself someday, but in the meantime, she flew across United States and back for "fun." She didn't know at the time that her transcontinental flight was also a first. She finally did fly solo across the Atlantic in 1932, the first woman to do so. She set four other world records for solo long distance flights in 1935, including a flight from Honolulu, Hawaii, to Oakland, California. She eventually gave up social work and devoted herself to writing, giving lectures, and providing career counseling for young women. She wanted her life to be an inspiration to other women to pursue whatever they desired to achieve, even if their goals appeared to be in a "man's" career.

By 1937, most of the "first to fly" records were achieved. Only one remained, and Amelia sought to establish it: she made plans to fly around the earth at the equator. Arrangements were made in advance around the world, and the press followed her every move. She and a navigator flew from west to east across Africa and Asia. U.S. Navy ships radioed to her as she began her flight over the Pacific. And then, all contact was lost after a final radio message from a point that indicated she was way off course. Her plane disappeared in a storm over the Pacific somewhere between New Guinea and the Howland Islands.

Air travel has become so commonplace that it is easy to lose sight of Amelia's accomplishments. In the 1920s and 1930s, planes were neither sophisticated nor well built, and just taking off was dangerous. In many of the planes, passengers and pilots sat in open cockpits and wore heavy leather jackets, scarves, helmets, and eye goggles. Planes rarely flew high, and numerous accidents occurred from hitting trees and hills. Furthermore, pilots had neither charts nor regular airports at which to land. When Amelia flew across the United States, she followed railroad tracks, roads, and rivers; and her map of the terrain was pinned to her jacket. On one leg of the trip, her map blew away, and she got lost. She finally found a road and followed it to a town, where she used main street as her landing strip.[29]

> **World changers are willing to take on new challenges in spite of personal danger.**
>
> •
>
> *Be of good courage, and he shall strengthen your heart.*
>
> Psalm 27:14 NKJV

THOMAS EDISON
(1847–1931)

❖

"An Inventor With An Eye For The Practical"

What would a logical person expect from a man who was branded by a schoolmaster as "retarded" and who finished only three months of formal education? Certainly not the versatile and inventive life of Thomas A. Edison!

Edison produced his first invention, an electric vote-recorder, when he was only twenty-one years old. It did not sell as Edison had hoped. He refused, however, to be discouraged and moved on to invent an improved stock ticker system. It *did* sell—for $40,000, a tremendous sum in the late nineteenth century. A series of other inventions followed, and Edison was soon both wealthy and famous. He didn't seem to notice, however. He was too busy inventing. He patented the phonograph in 1877 and the practical incandescent light in 1879.

He was not the first to invent an electric lighting system, but he was the first to develop a system of distributing electric power, which made electricity available for ordinary home use. In 1882, his company began producing electricity for homes in New York City, and the home use of electricity spread rapidly throughout the world thereafter. He later organized several industrial companies, including General Electric Company.

Among Edison's achievements, he contributed greatly to the development of motion-picture cameras and projectors; made significant improvements to the telephone, telegraph, and typewriter; and invented a dictating machine, a mimeograph machine, and a storage battery. In all, he patented more than a thousand separate inventions.

Early in his career, Edison set up a research lab at Menlo Park, New Jersey, where he employed a group of assistants to help him in his research. This became the prototype of large research laboratories that many industrial firms established later. He is credited with developing the concept of "corporate R&D"—in-house research and development divisions that employ scientific research teams to develop practical products.

What few people know about Edison is that for most of his life he suffered from seriously impaired hearing. He chose to compensate for his impairment in two ways: hard work and a focus on inventions that would either enhance his ability to hear or give him ample means of communicating apart from the spoken word.

Many of Edison's inventions were not "firsts" in a particular field, but rather, important enhancements that made creative inventions more usable. Edison sought to make the genius of others accessible and practical. In that, he succeeded as no other American has.

He continued to work with dogged persistence until his death at age eighty-four, well liked by those who knew him and an inspiration to other inventors and entrepreneurs who followed him.[30]

> **People who make concrete changes in the world also live and work in the practical world—not just the world of ideas.**
>
> •
>
> *[Wisdom]: Those who diligently seek me will find me.*
>
> Proverbs 8:17

ALBERT EINSTEIN
(1879–1955)

❧

"He Revolutionized Modern Science"

From childhood, Albert Einstein found himself curious about the "riddle of the huge world." He turned his curiosity toward the study of physics. After completing university studies, he worked as an office clerk by day and worked on his own ideas at night. In 1905, at age twenty-six, he began publishing scientific papers explaining his new theories. Some scoffed, especially when they learned he was not a university professor. Others were intrigued and began to test his hypotheses. Their observations confirmed his theories, and within sixteen years, he was a scientific superstar and winner of the Nobel Prize for science.

From the time Einstein's theories first gained notoriety, he found himself swept into world politics. He openly opposed World War I, and when the Nazi Party rose to power in Germany in the 1930s, he moved to the United States of America to become a professor at Princeton University. As a Jew, he used his influence to help thousands of Jews flee Europe and to work for the establishment of a Jewish homeland. David Ben-Gurion, first prime minister of Israel, asked him to be Israel's first president, and while Einstein felt honored, he refused, saying, "I am a scientist, not a politician."

Although Einstein is considered a genius, he was so slow in learning to talk that his parents were alarmed. In school, he was labeled a "misfit," his classmates avoided him, and he earned poor grades. He failed his first college entrance exam. Rather than complete routine assignments, he preferred to daydream about riding on a beam of light, and indeed, these daydreams led to the theory of relativity and his most famous formula: E=mc^2 (energy equals mass multiplied by the speed of light squared).

Einstein's theories about energy and mass were used by other scientists to create nuclear power. During World War II, when Einstein heard that the Nazis were developing atomic weapons based on his theories, he wrote to the president of the United States to warn him. Einstein had intended for his discoveries related to atomic power to be used for peaceful purposes, and he later voiced regret at their use for war. He said after World War II, "We have won the war, but we have not won the peace."

Throughout his life, Einstein was noted for quiet humility. When *Scientific American* magazine offered a $5,000 prize for the best explanation of relativity in 3,000 words, Einstein said, "I am the only one in my entire circle of friends who is not entering. I don't believe I could do it." He once gave this as his formula for success: "If *a* is success . . . I should say the formula is *a* equals *x* plus *y* plus *z, x* being work and *y* being play." And *z*? "Keeping your mouth shut."

A ten-year-old girl once visited Einstein regularly to receive help with her math homework. She explained, "People said that at No.

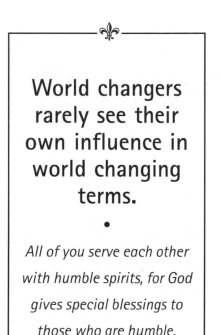

World changers rarely see their own influence in world changing terms.

•

All of you serve each other with humble spirits, for God gives special blessings to those who are humble.

1 Peter 5:5 TLB

112 there lives a very big mathematician, who is also a very good man. I asked him to help me. He was very willing and explained everything very well. He said I should come whenever I find a problem too difficult." When the mother apologized for her daughter's intrusion, Einstein said, "I have learned more from the conversations with the child than she has from me."[31]

FATHER FLANAGAN
(1886–1948)

❦

"He Founded a "'Town' to Shelter Forgotten Boys"

Edward Joseph Flanagan was born in Ireland, but at age eighteen, he moved to the United States and began to prepare for priesthood in the Roman Catholic Church. After training in Emmitsburg, Maryland; Rome; and Innsbruck; he was ordained in 1912 as a priest for the archdiocese of Omaha, Nebraska.

One main problem in Omaha that Father Flanagan found and chose to address personally: derelict boys. Many of these boys had no mothers, no fathers, and no homes. They had no one to love them or teach them right from wrong. Virtually all had dropped out of public school. They became known in the city for breaking store windows, being petty thieves (often stealing food), and starting street fights.

One day a grocer noted to Flanagan, "These boys should be arrested. They need to be taken away."

Looking beyond their vandalism Father Flanagan saw hungry faces and ragged clothes. He responded, "What they need is a home. They need someone to love them."

The grocer asked, "But who would take them in?"

He replied, "Maybe I will." And he did.

Father Flanagan borrowed a few dollars to rent an old house and then asked those in the immediate neighborhood to give him furniture, dishes, and bedding to furnish it and help fix it up. He invited five boys to move in with him, offering them a place to eat, sleep, play, and pray. Soon these boys were laughing, learning, and attending church regularly. The neighbors were impressed. More and more boys began coming to his door, eager for the normalcy of life he offered them. Father Flanagan finally concluded, "The boys need a town of their own."

In 1922, Father Flanagan found a farm for sale eleven miles outside Omaha, and again, he asked friends and neighbors to help with the purchase price and then to help build a town. They built streets, sidewalks, houses, shops, a church, and a post office. One large dining room was built as a place for the boys to eat, and a pool was constructed to give them a place to swim. Boys from across the nation began to arrive. One day a boy arrived in Boys' Town who could not walk, and Father Flanagan asked one of the older boys to carry him to his room. The big boy hoisted the newcomer onto his back as Father Flanagan asked, "He's not too heavy, is he?"

The older boy smiled and said, "He ain't heavy, Father. He's my brother!" The statement became the hallmark of Boys' Town. The action was immortalized in bronze, and the statement became a well-known quote across the nation.

Father Flanagan insisted that the entire "town" be devoted to developing character in homeless boys by giving them religious and social

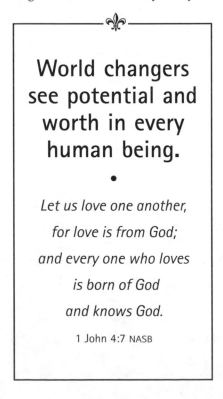

World changers see potential and worth in every human being.

•

Let us love one another, for love is from God; and every one who loves is born of God and knows God.

1 John 4:7 NASB

education, as well as vocational training. The institution was such a success that Father Flanagan became a sought-out authority on the training and reclamation of boys who had become juvenile delinquents. After World War II he served as a consultant to the United States government in setting up youth programs in Japan and Korea. He died while on a similar mission to Europe.[32]

ANNE FRANK
(1929–1945)

⚜

"Her Diary Put a Poignant Face Upon Racial Injustice"

Born in Germany in 1929, Anne Frank received a diary as a birthday present when she turned thirteen, and she made her first entry into it in June 1942, writing, "Kitty [which was the name she used to address her diary], I hope I shall be able to confide in you completely as I have never been able to do in anyone before, and I hope that you will be a great support and comfort to me." During the next two years, Anne wrote of her adolescence, including the dimension of terror and pity that haunted her world as the Nazis moved into her city, and Anne and her family were forced into hiding.

Anne's father, Otto Frank, was born in Frankfurt, Germany, where the Jewish community had contributed much to the city's commerce and culture. His family had been residents there since the seventeenth century, and he had served Germany as a lieutenant in World War I. After the war he became a banker. With Hitler's rise to power, he quickly realized that his past would not be his future and he moved the family to Amsterdam in 1933, establishing a food products business. War came to Holland in 1939, and in 1940, Germany conquered Holland. Anne wrote, "Good times rapidly fled."

Thousands of Jews were rounded up and sent to concentration camps in Germany. When the Frank family received a "call up" notice for Margot, Anne's older sister, the family went into hiding in a secret place they had prepared with the help of Otto's Dutch business associates. They lived there in hiding for two years, relying upon Dutch friends to bring them food and other necessities. Anne wrote of the political terror the family felt, but she mostly wrote honestly of her life as a young girl desiring a normal life of cycling, dancing, falling in love, and feeling young.

On August 4, 1944, the family members were discovered in their secret apartment and were led to Gestapo headquarters. A month later, with a thousand other Jews from Amsterdam, they were packed seventy-five to a freight car and sent on a train to Auschwitz concentration camp in Germany. At the time of the family's capture, the contents of a cupboard were emptied, including a stash of papers that was later recovered by one of the Dutch employees of the food company. Otto Frank survived Auschwitz, the only member of his family to do so, and he was given these papers when he returned to Amsterdam in 1945. Among the papers was Anne's diary. It was first published in Holland in 1947 as *The House Behind,* and very quickly, it was published in more than thirty languages around the world. The United States version of the diary, published in 1952 as *Anne Frank: The Diary of a Young Girl,* sold millions of copies and was made into a Pulitzer Prize-winning play and a movie.

Through the years, Anne's diary has caused millions of people to feel the preciousness of human life—with all of its possibilities and promises. She has come to be regarded as one of the most famous "voices" from the Holocaust and one of the greatest champions for racial justice in the twentieth century.[33]

> # World changers have an honesty that affects history when they tell their story.
>
> •
>
> *Thou hast put to shame those who hate us.*
>
> Psalm 44:7 NASB

Benjamin Franklin
(1706–1790)

❧

"A Founding Father Who Knew the Value Of Prayer"

Most people might not give a runaway with only two years of formal education much chance of succeeding in life, but that was the start of life for Benjamin Franklin.

One of seventeen children, Ben was largely self-educated, and after running away from an apprenticeship in the printing business, he worked in England and then moved to Philadelphia, where he founded his own printing business and newspaper. He often wrote under pseudonyms, including a character named "Silence Dogood" in Boston. "Poor Richard" was Ben's voice for expressing his thoughts on freedom, justice, and public spirit. *Poor Richard's Almanack,* which Ben not only wrote but also published, became the most widely read book after the Bible in the American colonies.

Franklin was a prolific writer, inventor, and student. Among his inventions were a stove that emitted more heat than a conventional fireplace, the lightning rod, bifocals, the gliding rocking chair, and a musical instrument he called the "armonica." Franklin never patented his inventions—he intended them for everyone's use.

Franklin was equally known as a leader and public-service innovator. He helped establish the first public library in North America, a police force, a volunteer fire department, a hospital, the first garbage collection service, and an academy that became the University of Pennsylvania.

He retired from his printing business at age forty-two to pursue his "hobbies." During this time, he learned French, Spanish, Italian, German, and Latin; continued to invent; became interested in electricity; and worked for the colonial government. He was sent by the colonies to England in 1757 in an attempt to convince England to uphold colonial rights. When he finally realized that England would not listen to colonial complaints, he returned home in 1775 to help draft the Declaration of Independence. At the end of the Revolution, he helped negotiate peace with England and became the first United States ambassador to France.

In the 1780s, he was called upon to help draft the U.S. Constitution. And it was in 1787 at the Constitutional Convention that Ben took one of his most courageous stands. The Convention was on the verge of failure over the issue of whether small states should have the same representation as large states. The deadlock seemed hopeless. At age eighty-one, Franklin rose with a suggestion. He was convinced that the Bible is right in saying, "Unless the Lord builds the house, its builders labor in vain" (Psalm 127:1), and he said: "Gentlemen, I have lived a long time and am convinced that God governs in the affairs of men. If a sparrow cannot fall to the ground without His notice, is it probable that an empire can rise without His aid? I move that prayer imploring the

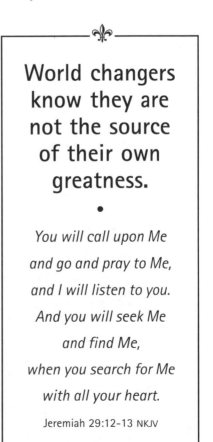

World changers know they are not the source of their own greatness.

•

You will call upon Me and go and pray to Me, and I will listen to you. And you will seek Me and find Me, when you search for Me with all your heart.

Jeremiah 29:12-13 NKJV

assistance of Heaven be held every morning before we proceed to business." The motion carried. And from then on prayer was offered each morning until a compromise was reached.[34]

GALILEO GALILEI
(1564–1642)

❧

"He Ushered in 'Science' as a Means of Understanding God's Universe"

An inventor, scholar, and researcher, Galileo is credited by historians as being the person who ushered in the scientific revolution. It was a revolution, however, that caused him great personal pain.

From his earliest years in Pisa and Florence, Galileo was interested in the natural world. The more he studied, the more he concluded that the inner workings of the universe could be revealed through patient study and research. In a work titled *On Motion,* he challenged the ideas of Aristotle. The book was not published, but it was circulated among his friends at the University of Pisa, where he was a professor of mathematics. What he wrote alarmed university officials as being too radical, and he was dismissed.

Galileo left Pisa so poor that he had to walk the final hundred miles to Padua to take a university position there. During his career, he invented the hydrostatic balance, the first practical thermometer, the geometric and military compass, the compound microscope, the "pulsilogia" (an instrument to measure the pulse), and the astronomical telescope. He became the first person to see the mountains on the moon, to discover the rings of Saturn, and to discover that the sun revolved and that the earth and planets revolved around the sun.

With opinions as revolutionary as his discoveries, Galileo's critics began to spread rumors that he was a heretic. He believed science had an important role in determining truth—an opinion that the Roman Catholic Church took as a direct challenge. Galileo traveled to Rome three times to win the pope's support for his work. The pope gave conditional approval, forcing Galileo to agree never to support Copernicus, who was the first to say the planets revolved around the sun.

In 1632, Galileo published *Dialogue Concerning the Two Chief World Systems.* The book challenged common teachings that two sets of unrelated natural laws governed heaven and earth. Galileo argued that humans and all things on earth were subject to natural laws, which physics and mathematics could describe. The book was published in Italian rather than Latin because Galileo wanted everyone to be able to read his work. The *Dialogue* was initially approved by Church authorities and was highly regarded by scientists and philosophers. The pope, however, had Galileo tried by the Inquisition for failing to keep their agreement. Galileo's books were banned, and he was placed under house arrest for the rest of his life. While under house arrest, he continued to write and to conduct research with pendulums. He died four years later.

In response to those who accused him of heresy Galileo

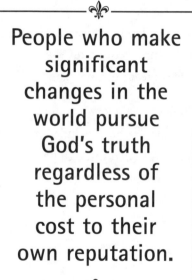

People who make significant changes in the world pursue God's truth regardless of the personal cost to their own reputation.

•

Those also who suffer according to the will of God shall entrust their souls to a faithful Creator in doing what is right.

1 Peter 4:19 NASB

said, "I do not think it necessary to believe that the same God who gave us our sense, our speech, our intellect, would have us put aside the use of these, to teach us instead such things as with their help we could find out for ourselves, particularly in the case of these sciences." He believed strongly that his ideas did not challenge the Church or the Bible, but rather that the truth could be found both in the Bible and nature. He wrote, "The Holy Bible and the phenomena of nature proceed alike from the Divine Word."[35]

John Glenn
(1921)

❧

"The First American Astronaut To Circle The Earth In Outer Space"

From early childhood, the boy the family called "Bud" enjoyed playing "airplane." With arms outstretched as wings, Bud Glenn would lead a "squadron" of his friends around the yard, making boyish airplane noises as they banked and dove. When an outbreak of scarlet fever confined him to his room for several weeks, John used balsa wood, a sharp knife, and a pot of glue to build model airplanes. He seemed born to fly.

After graduating from high school, both John and his childhood sweetheart, Annie, (who later became his wife) enrolled at Muskingum College. In addition to his course work as a chemical engineering major, John and four of his friends signed up for a government-sponsored civilian pilot training course at an airport in neighboring Tuscarawas County. John passed the course with high marks before progressing to his junior year of college. In his words, "I was sold on flying as soon as I had a taste for it."

Already a licensed flyer, John was quick to enlist in the military after Japanese planes bombed Pearl Harbor in 1941. Within two years, he had received his aviator's wings and a commission as a Marine second lieutenant. He flew fifty-nine dive-bombing missions on the Marshall Islands, logging more hours in the air during those missions than any other pilot in the squadron and earning the first of eighteen air medals. He decided to make the Marines his career.

Glenn served as a flight instructor, flew sixty-three fighter-bomber missions during the Korean War, and then entered Test Pilot School, where he became the first pilot to fly the new "Crusader" fighter on a transcontinental flight, setting a speed record with the flight. When NASA was formed in 1958, Glenn knew he fit part of NASA's profile for astronauts, but at age thirty-seven, he was considered old for the job. Nevertheless, he threw himself into preparing himself physically and mentally, determined to be among the first seven Mercury astronauts. He served as the back-up pilot for Alan Shephard's fifteen minutes in suborbital flight, and then on February 20, 1962, after eleven launch postponements and several holds in count-down, he flew *Friendship 7* into orbit around the earth, the first American to circle the earth in "outer space."

Knowing that his age made him an unlikely candidate for future Gemini and Apollo programs, Glenn retired from NASA, and for a brief time, he worked for Royal Crown Cola. Then after his friend Robert Kennedy was assassinated, he felt compelled to run for office, and in 1974, Glenn was elected as a Democratic senator from Ohio. He went on to serve five terms in the United States Senate.

Throughout the years, John Glenn made this statement to his wife, Annie, as he prepared to fly into harm's way: "Well, I'm going down to the corner drug store to

World changers often volunteer to serve, regardless of danger.

•

Then I heard the voice of the Lord, saying, "Whom shall I send, and who will go for Us?" Then I said, "Here am I. Send me!"

Isaiah 6:8 NASB

buy some gum." Her response was always, "Well, don't take too long."
That was their exchange as Glenn prepared, in 1998, to return to
space, this time as part of the *Discovery* Space Shuttle program. His
successful mission earned him the honor of being the oldest American
to go into space.[36]

BILLY GRAHAM
(1918)

❧

"Evangelist to The World"

At the time the Billy Graham evangelistic ministry was fully established—in the 1950s—the goal of Christianity for "evangelizing the world" was fading. Tensions between colonialism and national churches, as well as competition among missionary societies, had combined to diminish the vigor of Christian outreach. Communism and atheism were strong forces in many nations. Fifty years later, Communism had collapsed, and evangelism had again become a top priority of the Christian church. The central figure in this resurgence was Billy Graham.

In his life, Graham has preached to more people in person than anyone else in history—more than 210 million—with more than 2.8 million people responding to his invitation to "come forward" to accept Christ as Savior. More than 2.5 billion people in 160 nations are estimated to have heard his Easter Sunday sermon in April 1996, a televised message that was translated into forty-eight languages. From the 1950s onward, he has appeared in the annual Gallup-poll top-ten listing of "the most admired American." He is the speaker on an international radio network of more than a thousand stations and a columnist in newspapers with a combined circulation of more than 7 million readers. His books have been translated widely, with millions of copies sold. He received the Congressional Gold Medal in 1996 and was called "America's pastor" by President George Bush.

While Billy Graham's father prepared him to be a farmer, his mother insisted that her children memorize a Bible verse each day. His personal conversion to Christ came on the night before his sixteenth birthday during a revival crusade held in his hometown. He subsequently attended Florida Bible Institute and Wheaton College to prepare himself for ministry.

Early in his ministry, Graham made a statement that became a hallmark for his life: "I had one passion and that was to win souls." Youth for Christ International gave Graham his first national platform, but it was a telegram sent by newspaper giant William Randolph Hearst to "Puff Graham" that propelled Graham into national fame in the wake of the Los Angeles Campaign in 1949. A crusade in London in 1954 marked the beginning of his international evangelism efforts. He held major campaigns in India and the Far East (1956), Australia and New Zealand (1959), Berlin (1966), Nagaland (1972), Korea and South Africa (1973), and Poland (1977-78). He made his first official visit to Moscow in 1982 and to China in 1988. As a major watershed moment for evangelism, he convened the Lausanne Congress on World Evangelism in 1974. The collapse of Communism in 1991 opened the door for him to preach to fifty thousand Russians in Moscow's Olympic Stadium in 1992.

> # World changers allow themselves to be used by God for His purposes.
>
> •
>
> *You are to go into all the world and preach the Good News to everyone, everywhere.*
>
> Mark 16:15 TLB

Graham summed up his ministry in 1994 in a statement made after he had preached to the Queen of England and members of the royal family: "My job is to be faithful, to proclaim the Gospel wherever I am. It is always a time of tremendous soul searching, and great privilege, with a sense of humility and unworthiness, to preach the Gospel at any time."[37]

George Frederick Handel

(1685–1759)

❧

"His Music Brought a King to His Feet"

Toward the end of his life, George Frederick Handel, now regarded as one of the greatest names in the history of music, lost his health. His right side was paralyzed, his money was gone, and his creditors were threatening to imprison him. Handel was deeply disheartened. It was not at all the life he had known in earlier years.

Handel was born in Halle, Germany, and at the age of twelve made his debut as a performer at the court of Berlin. He later played in orchestras at Hanover and Hamburg, and it was while in Hamburg that he composed his first two operas. In 1706, at the age of twenty-one, he left Germany for Italy, where he studied three years and became widely known throughout the musical world for operas in the "Italian style." He then moved to England, where he remained the greater part of his life.

In England, Handel was appointed head of the Royal Academy of Music, and he changed from composing opera to composing oratorios. In fairly quick succession he produced *Israel in Egypt, L'Allegro* and *Il Penseroso, Saul, Samson,* and many other oratorios that gained great acclamation in England and across Europe. In all, he wrote some forty-two operas, as well as organ music, chamber concertos, sonatas, and songs. Two of his most popular works—*Water Music* and *Royal*

Fireworks Music were composed for holidays and outings promoted by the English royal court.

But then came 1741, and Handel, although only fifty-six years old, seemed worn out and depleted of music. He relied on his faith as he battled through his depression, and out of this dark period in his life, he created the work that became his most famous: *Messiah.* Handel shut himself away completely for twenty-three days as he composed *Messiah.* Meals brought to him were often untouched. At times during the composing of this masterpiece, friends found Handel sobbing with tears—he was so greatly moved by the biblical text and his love for Christ Jesus. He later said about his experience in writing "The Hallelujah Chorus," "I did think I did see all Heaven before me and the great God Himself."

Messiah premiered at a 1741 benefit for the Foundling Hospital in Dublin, but perhaps its most famous performance was in March of 1743, in London, an event attended by King George II. When the music reached its great "Hallelujah Chorus" climax, the king—greatly moved by emotion—rose to his feet as the words "For the Lord God omnipotent reigneth." All others in attendance quickly followed suit, standing as the lyrics honoring Jesus as "King of kings and Lord of lords" were sung. To this day, more than 250 years later, it is still the custom for audiences to rise as the chorus is being sung.

> ❦
>
> # World changers often act out of a faith tempered by the tests of life.
>
> •
>
> *The LORD is my strength and my song; he has become my salvation.*
>
> Exodus 15:2

After composing *Messiah,* Handel continued to work almost to the day of his death at age seventy-four, even though he was blind the last six years of his life. Few could match his energy.[38]

VÁCLAV HAVEL
(1936)

❧

"He Refused to Stop Voicing What He Believed"

Some people seem to retain their balance no matter how many times the foundation beneath them shakes. Václav Havel seems to be one such person.

When Havel was only twelve years old, his native Czechoslovakia fell to communism. His family's wealth was confiscated, his parents were forced to take low-paying jobs, and Václav was forbidden to attend regular schools. He refused to be counted among the uneducated, however, and after working all day, he went to school at night.

Although he worked at decidedly nonliterary jobs for much of his young life—first in factories and laboratories and later in the army—Havel always considered himself to be a writer and philosopher. In 1957, at age twenty-one and a student at a technical school, he was published in a literary magazine. In the army, he organized a theater troupe for his regiment. In his thirties, he became a playwright for a progressive theater company and published several plays.

Throughout the 1960s, Havel continued to write and publish essays and plays, many of which called into question the oppressive actions of the government. Then came the spring of 1968. The Soviet Union invaded Czechoslovakia to put an end to the reforms of Alexander Dubcek, the nation's leader. Havel called on the West to protest the human rights abuses, and the new Soviet-dominated Czech government responded by banning his works. Rather than flee the country, Havel worked in a brewery by day and continued to write at night. In 1978, after years of active dissent, he helped establish the Committee for the Defense of the Unjustly Persecuted. For that effort, he was arrested and sentenced to four years of hard labor.

Havel refused to be silenced. His prison letters to his wife Olga were published. In the 1980s he became an eloquent voice for freedom in Czechoslovakia. Unlike many other activists, however, he did more than simply condemn the repressive conditions in his nation. His message addressed government policies in the light of what it means to be a human being and to have a conscience, a soul. In January 1989, he was arrested again.

When released from prison the second time, Havel established the Civic Forum, a coalition of groups that sought a nonviolent approach to change. The result was the "Velvet Revolution," a bloodless collapse of communism in Czechoslovakia and the establishment of democracy. In December 1989, Havel was elected president of the newly formed Czech parliament. A year later, he authorized free elections and was re-elected president.

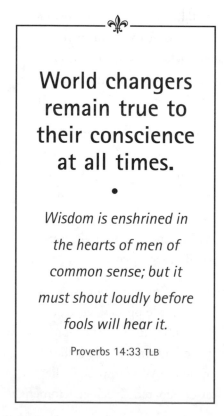

World changers remain true to their conscience at all times.

•

Wisdom is enshrined in the hearts of men of common sense; but it must shout loudly before fools will hear it.

Proverbs 14:33 TLB

In his first book after being elected president, Havel wrote this statement about one's duty to politics: "In all circumstances try to be decent, just, tolerant, and understanding; and at the same time try to resist corruption and deception.

In other words, I must do my utmost to act in harmony with my conscience and my better self." His words became the rallying cry of the Czech people as they rebuilt a free nation.[39]

MILTON HERSHEY
(1857-1945)

⚜

"He Built A Town On Chocolate"

Milton Hershey attended six different schools by the time he was thirteen because his family moved a great deal. His mother then decided it was time for him to learn a trade. His father, who loved reading, wanted Milton to stay in school. They reached a compromise: Milton became an apprentice to a printer, surrounded by the printed word. Milton, however, did not enjoy printing, and two years later he was apprenticed to a candy maker. At that time, candy was made without precise recipes. Milton discovered he had a special knack for candy making. Customers especially enjoyed his caramels, peppermints, and fudge. After a few years of apprentice work, Milton began his own candy business at age nineteen, in Philadelphia.

His uncle loaned him money to set up his first candy shop, but no matter how hard he worked, he soon had to admit his first business was a failure. He moved to Denver, hoping to succeed there. Again, he failed, although he did learn an important candy-making secret—fresh milk makes good candy. After Denver, Milton tried to succeed in candy shops in Chicago, New Orleans, and New York. No matter how hard he worked, he couldn't earn enough to pay his bills. He finally moved back to Pennsylvania—tired, broke, and discouraged.

His financial tide changed when Milton opened a small candy business in Lancaster, Pennsylvania. An Englishman was so impressed with his caramels made with fresh milk that he ordered a large supply shipped to England. Milton soon had more business than he could handle. Using original recipes, he expanded his line of candies, built factories in other Pennsylvania cities, and opened branches in New York City and Chicago. Caramels were shipped around the world.

In 1893, Milton visited the World's Columbian Exposition in Chicago and was drawn to an exhibition of chocolate-making equipment from Germany. He decided to shift his focus to chocolate making, and by 1900, his factory made 114 kinds of fancy chocolates. He sold his Lancaster Caramel Company in 1900 for a million dollars and built a new chocolate factory on farmland near his birthplace in Derry, Pennsylvania. People thought he was foolish to build a factory in the countryside, but Milton also wanted to build a town for his workers. Thus, Hershey, Pennsylvania, was born, with two main streets: Chocolate and Cocoa Avenues. Milton turned his growing fortune into schools, homes, churches, theaters, sports facilities, and an amusement park.

Milton focused on making just one kind of fancy candy in his new factory: a milk chocolate candy bar. In 1907 he developed the "Hershey Kiss," and other products were soon added. During World War II, he developed a special candy bar with added nutrients and vitamins for the soldiers. His chocolate factory eventually became the largest in the world.

He and his wife Kitty had no children of their own, but they had

> # World changers try and try again—until they succeed.
>
> •
>
> *If any man's work which he has built on it remains, he will receive a reward.*
>
> 1 Corinthians 3:14 NASB

a strong desire to help children. They used their vast wealth to establish an orphanage and school for boys. Today, the Milton Hershey School helps a thousand boys and girls.[40]

SIR EDMUND HILLARY
(1919)

⚜

"The First To Climb Everest"

The conditions atop Mount Everest, the world's highest peak, are among the harshest on planet Earth: sheer ice cliffs, deadly winds, waist-deep snow, bitter cold, sudden avalanches, limited visibility, and air so thin at 29,028 feet that oxygen masks are required. Harsh conditions, however, were no stranger to Edmund Hillary, the first man to reach Everest's summit.

As a child, Edmund walked barefoot to school, no matter the weather. His strict parents, who were farmers and beekeepers, believed that every physical disorder was caused by overeating. The cure, therefore, was dieting. Edmund's teachers often told him bluntly that he was physically unfit, thin, weak, and too often sick.

Sometimes reading at the rate of a book a day, Edmund escaped his harsh family life through adventure stories. Then, at sixteen, he went skiing for the first time. He not only felt intoxicated by the sight of snow, but upon eavesdropping on a conversation by a group of mountain climbers, he came away from the trip with a decision, "I must climb something!"

Edmund began to spend all of his free time hiking, jogging, and climbing mountains. He broke three ribs in one fall, was gored by a frightened yak during another climb, and suffered infected leech bites, massive blisters, and frozen nose drips on various climbs—but he was determined to face and master all of the major mountain-climbing goals he set for himself. In 1953, that goal was Everest. With a native sherpa from Nepal, Tenzing Norgay, Hillary planned and conquered the ultimate mountain challenge, reaching the summit just seconds before Norgay. They celebrated by eating a small mint cake and taking photographs. Edmund left a crucifix on the summit that he had worn during the climb.

The fact that his climb brought him celebrity status surprised Hillary. He still thought of himself as a beekeeper carrying on his parents' business. His first response to fame was to buy a new pair of pants to wear in public. He was invited to give lectures around the world, and he found that he enjoyed this new challenge. He joined an expedition to the South Pole in 1958 and became the first person since Scott to reach that destination. He also undertook expeditions in search of the mythical "abominable snowman" but concluded that the creature did not exist although a rare Tibetan blue bear did! Through the years, his wife and three children often joined him on his expeditions. He wrote numerous books about his travels—adventure stories not unlike the ones he had enjoyed as a boy. Through his expeditions and books, he inspired countless people to take physical risks and attempt great challenges.

World changers never stop short of reaching their goals.

•

Do you not know that those who run in a race all run, but one receives the prize? Run in such a way that you may obtain it.

1 Corinthians 9:24 NKJV

After the death of his wife and youngest daughter, killed in a plane crash, Edmund began to devote his life to working in hospitals and helping build schools and bridges to improve the lives of the Himalayan people. He was knighted by the Queen of England, not only for his bravery, but also for his humanitarian work.[41]

KING JAMES I
(1566–1625)

⚜

"He Approved The Creation Of The World's Most Popular Version Of The Bible"

James I of England, who was also James VI of Scotland, was the only son of Mary, Queen of Scots. When he was a year old, his mother was forced to abdicate her throne, and James was crowned king and placed in the protective custody of Scottish lords. He had a number of famous childhood tutors, including George Buchanan, a notable Presbyterian minister, and he became proficient in theology. He was given nominal control of the government at age thirteen.

In 1603, James succeeded Queen Elizabeth I, inheriting the throne because both his mother and father were great grandchildren of Henry VII. He embraced his larger kingdom with enthusiasm to achieve peace abroad and religious toleration at home. He settled England's war with Spain, modified laws against Roman Catholics in England, and opened a dialog aimed at reform of the state church of England.

England had two competing Bibles at the time James I became king: the Bishops' Bible preferred by church authorities; and the Geneva Bible favored by the people. James I called a conference of theologians and church leaders at Hampton Court in 1604 "for the hearing, and for the determining, things pretended to be amiss in the Church." Puritan John Reynolds proposed a new translation of the Bible be made to replace the two existing ones. The king approved the plan, ordering "a translation be made of the whole Bible, as consonant as can be to the original Hebrew and Greek, and this is to be set out and printed without any marginal notes and only to be used in all Churches of England in time of Divine Service."

Fifty-four scholars were involved in the work, which was begun in 1606. The Bishop's Bible was considered the primary text, but a provision was made to use the Tyndale, Matthew, Coverdale, Whitchurch, and Geneva texts whenever "they agree better with the Text." The translation was published in 1611 and immediately went through several editions as changes were made to refine it.

Although the new Bible text was never formally authorized by either King James I or Parliament, it became known as the "Authorized Version." It took nearly forty years, however, before it replaced the Geneva Bible as a favorite among the people. Once it was established, it became the Bible of the English-speaking world. It continues to be one of the most widely read Bibles in English, and through the centuries, more copies of it have been published and distributed than any other version of the Bible.

The 1611 Bible was perhaps the most important lasting result of James I's rule. Through the later years of his reign, he had ongoing disputes with Parliament over the amount of money he could spend on royal pursuits. He continued to face opposition among England's leaders for his foreign policies that

---

Genuine world changing goes hand-in-hand with righteous leadership.

•

My hands also will I lift up unto thy commandments, which I have loved; and I will meditate in thy statutes.

Psalm 119:48 KJV

accommodated Roman Catholic powers. During the last years of his reign, England also became embroiled in a series of expensive and fruit-less wars.

James I was not only king, but also an author. He wrote extensively on matters related to the monarchy and theology. He specifically denounced the dangers of tobacco smoking and the practice of witchcraft.[42]

JOAN OF ARC
(1412-1431)

❧

"She Did What God Asked Of Her"

As a young peasant girl, she was simply known as "Jeanne." She grew up in a part of France that was being ravaged by the English and their allies from Burgundy, while the dauphin of France, Charles VII, remained uncrowned because the traditional place of investiture, Reims, was held by France's enemies.

A deeply religious girl, Joan often took refuge in the local church at Arc for prayer. There, she began to experience visions of saints and to hear Heavenly voices urging her to take up arms to save France. She became convinced that she was the "Maiden," a person who had been prophesied in years past as a young woman who would restore the glory of France.

Boldness in leading others to win small skirmishes against the enemy earned her the respect of French loyalists, and in 1429, she made a bold trip to visit the dauphin. Word of her claim to be able to save the nation by means of special orders from God had preceded her to the court at Chinon. The dauphin was impressed that she had even survived the dangerous journey through territory held by the powerful English armies, and he reluctantly agreed to an audience with her. He decided, however, to put her claims of spiritual power to an early test. He gave all signs of his royal office to another and stood unceremoniously with other courtroom guests to await her arrival.

Joan entered the room dressed in the garments of a man and walked directly to the true dauphin, not the impostor. She dropped on one knee before him, and he, in amazement, immediately agreed to a private conversation with her. She then told him of a prayer he had prayed several months before in secret and in silence. She described the prayer using the exact words he had used, and she gave him God's answer. He took courage at her words and began to make renewed plans to combat France's invaders.

A captain's commission was eventually awarded to Joan, who took on the armor of a man and placed herself in the thickest part of military conflict. She led a successful battle to break the siege of Orleans, at which point she became known as the "Maid of Orleans." The nearly captive nation took great courage at her feat, and the troops began to rally in their effort to drive the English and Burgundians from their soil. The eventual coronation of Charles VII at Reims was considered a turning point in the war.

Joan d'Arc was unsuccessful in liberating Paris. She was captured in early 1430 by the Burgundians, who turned her over to Bishop Pierre Cauchon to be tried for witchcraft and heresy. Under great pressure from Cauchon, who had taken the English side, she maintained her innocence. Finally, in exhaustion, she signed an admission of heresy and was imprisoned, but then she withdrew her statement and reaffirmed her innocence. She eventually was turned over to secular authorities and was burned at the stake in 1431.

> **World changers often are called and willing to make personal sacrifices.**
>
> •
>
> *We cannot but speak the things which we |have seen and heard.*
>
> Acts 4:20 NKJV

Twenty-five years later, new proceedings annulled the trial and verdict. In 1920, she was named a saint. She is the patron saint of France.

To believers around the world, Joan of Arc is championed as a hero for one singular fact: she was willing to risk her life to deliver a message from God.[43]

POPE JOHN PAUL II
(1920)

❧

"International Advocate Of Human Dignity In Christ"

When Karol Jozef Wojtyla, the archbishop of Krakow, Poland, was selected to become pope in 1978—taking the name John Paul II in honor of his predecessor John Paul I who died just thirty-two days in office—his election made history. He was the first non-Italian to be pope in 456 years and the only Pole ever elected to the highest office in the Roman Catholic Church.

Known by his friends as energetic and deeply spiritual, he displayed a passionate interest in the entire spectrum of human life: spiritual, economic, physical, and political. In his life prior to becoming a priest, he experienced the death of beloved family members and friends, had jobs that were both menial and hard physically, attended university and was a student activist, and was a published playwright (all three of his plays based on biblical themes: *David, Job,* and *Jeremiah)*.

As Pope, John Paul II has traveled to more nations and logged more miles than any pope in history. "Christ," however, has been the theme of his papacy. He set that tone in his inaugural sermon, saying, "Brothers and sisters, don't be afraid to welcome Christ and to accept his power."

During his papacy, he has had great impact on the international stage. He played a decisive role in the collapse of Communism in Europe in the 1980s and has been a major influence on spiritual life in Cuba. He was the first pope to receive a visit from a Soviet leader, Mikhail Gorbachev, who

117

said after their meeting, "We have changed our attitude. Moral values that religion generated and embodied for centuries can help in the renewal of our country too." He has done more than any other pope to mend relations with the Jewish people and in 1996, became the first pope to enter a synagogue in Rome since the apostle Peter. In 2000, he publicly prayed for forgiveness for the Church's failure through the centuries to combat atrocities against Jews, native Americans, women, homosexuals, children abused by priests, and other maligned groups of people.

The most culturally and geographically diverse group of Catholic leaders in history have been promoted to cardinal by John Paul II. By 1996, he had named half of the world's 4,200 Catholic bishops and 100 of the 120-member college of cardinals, two-thirds of them from Third World nations. He has sought to uphold human dignity in all forms, speaking strongly against abortion, euthanasia, poverty, bigotry, and the dehumanizing aspects of materialism. Although he is compassionate to the disenfranchised, he has remained highly confrontational to those who desire to open the priesthood to women and married clergy.

Perhaps first and foremost, John Paul II has been a man of prayer. He begins each day at 6:15 in his private chapel in prayer, often in intense intercession. He has said, "When I was young, I thought that prayer could be—should be—only in thankfulness and adoration. . . . I changed my opinion completely. Today I ask very much."

> ❧
> # World changers both pray and act.
> •
> *The road of the godly leads upward.*
> Proverbs 15:24 TLB

Billy Graham has said of Pope John Paul II: "He's the strong conscience of the whole Christian world."[44]

HELEN KELLER
(1880-1968)

❧

"Courage To Conquer Her World"

"The two most interesting characters of the nineteenth century are Napoleon and Helen Keller." That was the opinion that Mark Twain voiced about Helen Keller when she was only fifteen years old. He reasoned that Napoleon failed to conquer his world as he intended, but Keller conquered hers. Keller traded in the titles of "blind, deaf, and mute" given to her as a child for the titles of scholar, philosopher, author, motion picture actress, traveler, lecturer, and winner of countless awards and accolades.

Born a normal child in every way, Keller was diagnosed with "acute congestion of the stomach and brain" at nineteen months old and suffered a fever that took her to the brink of death. When the fever broke, the disease was gone but so were her abilities to see, hear, and speak. Experts predicted a life "doomed to a void of eternal dark silence."

Keller, however, refused to relinquish her curiosity about the world or her desire to communicate. Her attempts at communication prompted her to overturn the baby carriage in which her baby sister was sleeping and shortly thereafter, to catch her apron on fire by the family hearth. Alarmed by these behaviors, her parents sought help, including the counsel of Alexander Graham Bell. A year later, the search for a teacher ended when Anne Mansfield Sullivan became Keller's mentor and friend and taught her to make an association with objects and letters that were "fingered" into her hand. Within months, Keller's remarkable progress had attracted the interest of educators nationwide.

Unwilling to limit her communication to reading and writing Braille and "raised print," Keller began to take speech lessons and eventually learned to speak not only English, but also French and German. She successfully completed courses in Latin, Greek, and Roman history, and she earned honors in English and German. In 1900, she entered Radcliffe College.

During her life, Keller lectured in every state of the union, speaking mainly on the needs of the blind and raising funds to help found the National Committee for the Prevention of Blindness. She also helped create the American Foundation for the Blind. She wrote a number of books and essays, and she made a motion picture of her life.

Somewhat ironically, one of the most famous quotes attributed to Keller is this: "Keep your face to the sunshine and you cannot see the shadows."

> # World changers pursue the Light, even when they are denied physical light.
>
> •
>
> *Even the darkness is not dark to Thee.*
>
> Psalm 139:12 NASB

"Helen Keller," wrote her friend Edward Everett Hale, a poet and teacher, "cannot see the written word in the stars, in the ocean, in the green grass, in the violet, or the dandelion. She cannot hear the spoken word in the song of the bluebird or the cricket or the peep-frog or the thunder or the surf on the shore. But none the less she does know what is the omnipotence of God, what is the infinite range of hope, and what is faith in the unseen."[45]

MARTIN LUTHER KING JR.
(1929–1968)

❦

"His Dream Inspired An Entire Nation To Face Its Racial Prejudice"

Martin Luther King Jr. was born the son of a prominent Baptist minister and grew up in a thirteen-room house in the best black neighborhood of Atlanta without experiencing many of the indignities that poorer blacks suffered. He also grew up in a home that was active in resisting anti-black biases, and he was raised to believe that quality of character, not race, should be the basis on which a person is judged.

As a boy, he enjoyed sports, jitterbugging, nice clothes, and girls. He was also an excellent student, skipping two grades in high school. At age fifteen, he entered Morehouse College. He considered becoming a doctor or lawyer, but in the end, he chose the family tradition of ministry. He was ordained immediately after graduation from college and was elected co-pastor of his father's church. He later enrolled at Crozer Theological Seminary in Chester, Pennsylvania, where he was only one of six blacks in a class of one hundred students. He graduated as president and valedictorian of his class and went on to Boston University to earn a Ph.D. in systematic theology in 1955. He also took courses in philosophy at Harvard, and while in Boston, he met and married Coretta Scott.

After Boston, King took a position as pastor of the Dexter Avenue Baptist Church in Montgomery, Alabama. Shortly after his arrival, Rosa

Parks took a seat in the "white" section of a city bus and refused the driver's orders to move to the "black" section. Her arrest and the subsequent bus boycott that lasted for 381 days, brought Martin Luther King into the national limelight. He was active in urging blacks to "protest courageously, and yet with dignity and love." He was arrested in Birmingham after leading a civil rights march, and while in jail, he wrote a 9,000-word statement about racial justice that truly marked him as the recognized leader of the civil rights movement. His famous "I Have a Dream" speech was delivered in front of the Lincoln Memorial during the Freedom March in Washington, D.C., on August 28, 1963. In 1964, President Lyndon Johnson signed the Civil Rights Bill, which opened public facilities to black people and desegregated public accommodations. In October 1964, King received the Nobel Peace Prize.

In areas of the South where blacks were denied the right to vote, King continued to lead marches. In 1965, Congress passed the Voting Rights Act. King then turned his attention to poverty. He began plans for a Poor People's March on Washington, D.C. While planning this event, King went to Memphis, Tennessee, where predominantly black sanitation workers were on strike for higher wages. There, while standing on his motel room's balcony, he was assassinated by a sniper's bullet. He was only thirty-nine years old.

> # World changers are willing to risk their life to do God's will.
>
> •
>
> *Do you want to be unafraid*
> *of the authority?*
> *Do what is good, and you will*
> *have praise for the same.*
>
> Romans 13:3 NKJV

Throughout his life, King advocated a course of nonviolent protest. He said as part of his final speech in Memphis, "We've got some difficult days ahead. But it really doesn't matter with me now. Because I've been to the mountaintop. . . . Like anybody I would like to live a long life . . . but I'm not concerned with that now; I just want to do God's will. I may not get there with you, but I want you to know tonight that we as a people will get to the Promised Land."[46]

ANNA LEONOWENS
(1834–1914)

❧

"She Changed A Nation By Educating A Child"

Anna Leonowens would no doubt have been very surprised that her life resulted in a book, a Broadway musical, an animated film, a television serial, and more than one major motion picture. She saw herself simply as a young Welsh woman who became a widow and a single mother at an early age. At age fifteen, she had gone with her family to Asia, where she met and married Major Thomas Lewis Leonowens of the Indian Army. Her husband died in 1858, and after living for a while in Singapore, she returned to England to enroll her older daughter in school.

When the call was put out for a teacher and governess in the palace of King Mongkut (Rama IV) of Siam—as the nation of Thailand was known in the 1800s—Anna believed that God was calling her to this unusual post. She wrote in her diaries that she felt a great kinship with Esther of the Old Testament, whose favor with a king affected the course of history. She applied for the position of governess to the royal children, and in 1862, at the invitation of the king, she embarked with her younger son for the post. For five years, she was part of the royal household in Bangkok.

During the years that Leonowens was in Siam, she was repulsed by the slavery she encountered. Accounts vary as to whether her judgment of the Siamese court life was exaggerated or justified, but from

Anna's own diaries, her disdain for the cruel treatment of Siamese "slaves" is clear.

King Mongkut prohibited Anna from trying to convert the children of the palace to Christianity, and he forbade her from speaking out against any social customs or traditions she saw in Siam. He sharply restricted her role to teaching the children to read, write, and speak English clearly, and to learn enough geography to be wise rulers of the nation. What the king did not curtail, however, were her methods or her textbooks, and Leonowens turned to Bible stories as her texts for teaching the children English, and in the process, biblical values. She especially focused her teaching on Crown Prince Chulalongkorn.

On the day he became king, Chulalongkorn made an amazing proclamation: his subjects would no longer be required to prostrate themselves in human worship in front of him or to crawl on hands and knees in his presence. Later in his reign, he outlawed slavery and the practice of imprisoning wives and children to repay the debts of their husbands and fathers. He also encouraged Christian missionaries to start hospitals and schools in Siam.

Eventually Leonowens returned to Great Britain and then later immigrated to Canada. She had an opportunity to meet Chulalongkorn in New York after he had been king for several years. He told her he had formed his

> ## Great world changers teach world—changing principles to others—even under opposition.
>
> •
>
> *The King's heart is like channels of water in the hand of the LORD; He turns it wherever He wishes.*
>
> Proverbs 21:1 NASB

plans for transforming his kingdom based upon the principles she had taught him.

Leonowens wrote two books about her experiences in Siam: *The English Governess at the Siamese Court* (1870) and *The Romance of the Harem* (1872). Her adventures inspired a popular book by Margaret Landon, *Anna and the King of Siam* (1944) on which Richard Rodgers and Oscar Hammerstein II based a musical, *The King and I*.[47]

C. S. LEWIS
(1898–1963)

✣

"He Became One Of The Major Christian Writers Of His Century"

Clive Staples Lewis was born in a small Irish town near Belfast in 1898. After serving in the military and being wounded in France during World War I, he returned to Oxford University to complete his education. He was elected Fellow of Magdalen College in 1925, and he spent the rest of his working life, from 1925 to 1962, at the universities of Oxford and Cambridge, tutoring two generations of students in medieval and Renaissance literature. He wrote numerous books during those years, including theological writings, children's books, science fiction, and scholarly works.

A long-standing bachelor, Lewis nonetheless acquired two "families." While training for World War I, he befriended Paddy Moore and volunteered to take care of Paddy's mother if he did not return from the war. Paddy was killed in action, and Lewis looked after Mrs. Moore and her daughter, Maureen, until Mrs. Moore died in 1949. In 1957, he acquired another family, this time marrying a dying divorcee from New York, Joy Davidsman Gresham. She and her two sons joined Lewis and his brother, Warren, at his home, "The Kilns," until her death in 1960.

With friend and colleague on Oxford's English faculty, J. R. R. Tolkien, Lewis added writing to his teaching. He desired to be a poet but failed to gain popularity in that genre. He then wrote children's stories, collectively called *The Chronicles of Narnia.* Among his spiritual works, he is perhaps best known for *The Screwtape Letters, Mere Christianity,* and *The Problem of Pain.*

As a young man, Lewis thought of himself as an atheist, but while reading in his university rooms at the age of twenty-eight, he had a conversation with a colleague Thomas Dewar Weldon that set him on a spiritual search that ended three years later. Lewis wrote, "I gave in, and admitted that God was God, and knelt and prayed: perhaps, that night, the most dejected and reluctant convert in all England." Several months later, he wrote to a friend, "I have just passed on from believing in God to definitely believing in Christ—in Christianity." By the end of 1931, Lewis was going to church, praying regularly, and taking communion regularly. He shortly thereafter began to give sermons, a number of which were broadcast nationally in England and later collected into books.

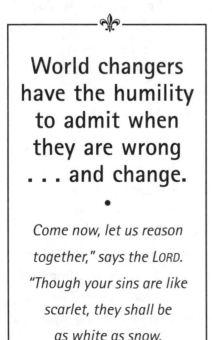

World changers have the humility to admit when they are wrong . . . and change.

•

Come now, let us reason together," says the LORD. *"Though your sins are like scarlet, they shall be as white as snow.*

Isaiah 1:18 NIV

His reputation as a teacher and writer continued to grow in the years after his death. Lewis's stories, including his life stories, were translated to film and video. His writings became the subject of literature courses and were woven into church curriculum. He gained a reputation as the "scholar pilgrim"—a man who did not perceive that logic and faith were enemies, but rather, that logic was a legitimate path toward faith. He was willing to admit when a long-held philosophy did not stand up to soundly reasoned Christian apologetics.

C. S. Lewis died on the same day John F. Kennedy was assassinated and Aldous Huxley died. His death received little notice on the world stage, but in the years since, his life has been remembered with increasing respect and admiration.[48]

ERIC LIDDELL
(1902–1945)

❧

"He Ran For The Prize Of The Highest Calling"

"That boy will never be able to run again." So said Mrs. Smith, a neighbor of the Liddell family at the Siaochang mission house in the aftermath of little Eric's bout with a high fever. Eric was to prove her wrong . . . very wrong.

At age five, Eric returned with his family to their native Scotland for a furlough, and the next year, he and his older brother, Robert, entered the School for Sons of Missionaries while his parents returned to China. The school's headmaster believed strongly that sports were good for boys, and Eric quickly developed a physique that enabled him to play several bruising rugby matches a week. Soon, Eric and Robert were monopolizing first and second places in school sports.

Upon graduation, Eric entered a university athletic program. Although his legs were stiff from a cycle tour of the Highlands, he surprised everyone by winning the 100-meter dash in a national meet. He was edged out by a slim margin in the 220 meters. It was the only race he ever lost in Scotland.

In his final year at the university Eric gave up rugby and concentrated on running, filling his sister's house with trophies for the sport. Meanwhile, Eric's parents knew little of his track success because he rarely wrote of his victories. Instead, he wrote about things that were truly important to him: he had joined a Bible class at school, became a member of the Church of Scotland, and became a founding member of a Crusader's Christian Union. Because of his track feats and his policy of always shaking the hands of an opponent before a race, he was invited to speak often about his faith. Although he had little public-speaking ability, his messages were well received because of his sincere desire for others to know God as he did.

The showdown for Eric's faith came during the 1924 Olympics when one of his events, the 100-meter dash, was scheduled for Sunday. Eric refused to run on the Sabbath, a decision that caused him to be accused of being narrow-minded and a traitor. The athletic authorities offered him the 400-meter race instead, along with his customary 200-meter. He won the bronze medal for the 200 meters but was given little chance to even place in the 400 meters since he had never run that race in international competition. Moments before the race, a team masseur handed him a note that read, "In the old book it says, '[He] that honors me, I will honor.'" Eric knew the statement was a biblical reference (1 Samuel 2:30), and he entered the race confident that win or lose, God would be honored. Eric flew around the track to the amazement of all who saw him run, and he not only won the gold medal, but also set a new world record.

The following year, Eric left Scotland, and for the next twenty

> **World changers remain true to their inner convictions— regardless of outer temptations for fame and glory.**
>
> •
>
> *Blessed is the man who refuses to work during my Sabbath days of rest, but honors them; and blessed is the man who checks himself from doing wrong.*
>
> Isaiah 56:2 TLB

years, he worked as a missionary in rural China. He was imprisoned by the Japanese for aiding wounded Chinese soldiers, and he died in the Weihsien prison camp two years later of a brain tumor. While in the camp, he energetically taught children and organized athletic activities, all in service to His Savior and Lord.[49]

ABRAHAM LINCOLN
(1809–1865)

⚜

"He Fought To Preserve The Union"

Abraham Lincoln knew a great deal about loss. His mother died when he was nine; he lost an election to the Illinois state legislature (1832), failed to obtain a desired appointment as Commissioner of the General Land Office in Illinois (1849), lost Senate races (1855, 1858), lost a vice presidential nomination (1856); and in 1864, he seemed on the verge of losing a bid for a second term as president. In 1850, his four-year-old son died; in 1851, his father died; and in 1862, his twelve-year-old son died. Few people, however, remember Lincoln's losses because his victories were so important.

Born in a log cabin in Kentucky, Lincoln attended only a few months of "blab school"—a school with no books at which the students repeated the teacher's words aloud. He moved with his family to southwest Indiana and then later to Illinois. He became a captain in the Black Hawk War and was elected to the Illinois state legislature in 1834. Along the way, he taught himself mathematics, read classical literature, and worked on his writing style. He took the Bible as his model for writing and speaking, and he disciplined himself to produce crisp, clear, simple sentences. He once said, "I will study and prepare myself, and one day when the time comes, I will be ready." He wrote to a friend, "Always bear in mind that your own resolution to succeed is more important than any other one thing."

Lincoln worked as a general store shopkeeper for a while, a venture that went bankrupt and left Lincoln owing $1,100, a tremendous sum in those days. He promised to pay it all. It took him fifteen years, but he kept his word. Lincoln began his law practice in 1836; when his clients overpaid him, he sent refunds. People in the area began to call him "Honest Abe."

As a state legislator, Lincoln took his first stand against slavery. His stand was not popular—only five lawmakers sided with him, and seventy-seven sided with the slave owners in a key vote about slavery. He became the first president ever elected without an electoral vote from a slave state. By the time Lincoln took office, the Confederacy had declared its existence, and the Civil War began his first year in office.

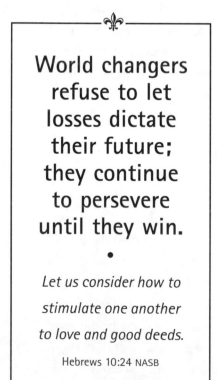

World changers refuse to let losses dictate their future; they continue to persevere until they win.

•

Let us consider how to stimulate one another to love and good deeds.

Hebrews 10:24 NASB

A major turning point of the Civil War came with victories at Gettysburg and Vicksburg. Lincoln was asked by his generals on the eve of the Gettysburg battle why he was so calm. He answered, "I spent last night in prayer before the Lord. He has given to me the assurance that our cause will triumph and that the nation will be preserved." Lincoln's "Gettysburg Address" is considered one of the most outstanding political speeches in American history. It was only five days after General Lee surrendered—on the evening of Good Friday in 1865—that Lincoln was shot while attending a performance at Ford's Theater.

Throughout his life, Lincoln was unwavering in his desire to do what was right and to do his best. He once said during the Civil War, "I do the very best I know how; the very best I can; and I mean to keep on doing it to the end. If the end brings me out all right, what is said against me will not amount to anything. If the end brings me out all wrong, then a legion of angels swearing I was right will make no difference."[50]

CHARLES A. LINDBERGH
(1902–1974)

✣

"He Opened A New Frontier"

In 1919, Raymond Orteig offered a prize of $25,000 for the first nonstop airplane flight between New York and Paris. The race was on! Several died attempting the crossing, and in the spring of 1927, events came to a climax. A French flying ace had an accident at takeoff, and a short while later, two aviators met their death somewhere over the North Atlantic. Explorer Richard Byrd spoke periodically about making an attempt. Then, a twenty-five-year-old unknown entered the stage: Charles A. Lindbergh.

As a barnstorming and mail pilot, Lindbergh had faced death before, bailing out of disabled planes on four occasions. He announced a solo attempt, trained to stay alert forty hours at a stretch, and had excellent maps. Few gave him much of a chance of succeeding, however.

After one bad-weather delay, he took off May 2, 1927 and arrived thirty-three and a half hours later at Le Bourget Airport in Paris. Americans followed news of his flight in *The Spirit of St. Louis* with eager expectation and seemed overwhelmed at his feat of skill and courage. Four million people lined New York City streets for a ticker tape parade, and Lindbergh quickly became a hero in demand—lucrative endorsements and public appearances were offered to him, nearly 5,000 poems were written about him, a Colorado mountain was named in his honor, and he received countless awards, including the Distinguished Flying Cross.

Lindbergh did not enjoy the publicity, but he was hounded by it the rest of his life. In 1929, he married Anne Morrow, an author who accompanied him on many of his later flights. Sadly, the Lindberghs made international headlines in 1932, when their two-year-old son was kidnapped and murdered. After his death, the Lindberghs moved to England for five years. There, Lindbergh was active in the America First Committee as an isolationist. He resigned his Air Corps Reserves commission but accompanied combat missions during World War II as a consultant to an aircraft manufacturer. In 1954, he was made brigadier general in the Air Force Reserve. Lindbergh also became an author and received the Pulitzer Prize for his book, *The Spirit of St. Louis.*

Part of the reason for Lindbergh's popularity was his all-American-boy image. In the jazz and nightclub era, he stood in sharp contrast as a serious, hard-working young man who had a passion for tinkering with machines, didn't smoke or drink, and who was modest even in the face of great adulation.

Lindbergh once said, "In my youth, science was more important to me than either man or God. I worshipped science. . . . Now I understand that spiritual truth is more essential to a nation than the mortar in its cities' walls. For when the actions of a

> **World changers grow and mature beyond the events that first brought them public notice.**
>
> •
>
> *He will teach the ways that are right and best to those who humbly turn to him.*
>
> Psalm 25:9 TLB

137

people are undergirded by spiritual truths, there is safety. When spiritual truths are rejected, it is only a matter of time before civilization will collapse. We must understand spiritual truths and apply them to our modern life. We must draw strength from the almost forgotten virtues of simplicity, humility, contemplation, and prayer. It requires a dedication beyond science, beyond self, but the rewards are great and it is our only hope."[51]

DAVID LIVINGSTONE
(1813-1873)

⚜

"He Helped Bring An End To Slave Traffic In Africa"

David Livingstone had no real childhood. He, his parents, and four brothers and sisters, lived in a ten-by-fourteen-foot one-room apartment in a Glasgow tenement. At age ten, he went to work in the cotton mills, twelve-and-a-half hours a day, six days a week. He was determined, however, not to spend his entire life in the mills. At the end of each work day, he attended an evening school sponsored by the mill owners. He studied Latin, botany, theology, and math. On his day off, he wandered the countryside, collecting rocks and plants for his own science studies.

Raised in a religious family, David saw a pamphlet describing the need for a new kind of missionary—one trained in medicine—he felt called to take on the challenge. By age twenty-one, he had been accepted for training by the London Missionary Society, and he was enrolled at Anderson's College in Glasgow. His desire was to be a missionary in China, but since China and England were at war when he qualified as a doctor, the Society sent him to Africa. There, in 1841, he began his work in what is now Botswana. He wrote: "I hope . . . to work as long as I live beyond other men's line of things and plant the seed of the Gospel where others have not planted." He did just that.

Livingstone became the first white person to see Lake Ngani and Victoria Falls. On his journeys, he confronted rampant slave trading—

tribes selling captives from other tribes to Arab traders who supplied the slave market owned by the Sultan of Zanzibar. Livingstone wrote that "the great disease [of Africa] is broken-heartedness," and he developed a plan to entice merchants from England to central Africa with a hope that legitimate trade would chase out slave trade. He drew worldwide attention to his goal by making a transcontinental walk from the Atlantic Ocean east to the mouth of the Zambezi River in Mozambique.

The rest of his life Livingstone explored central Africa. In 1871, several years after the western world began to question whether he was still alive, a foreign correspondent for two New York newspapers, Henry Morton Stanley, was sent in search of Livingstone. He found him in Ujiji, a trading center on the eastern shore of Lake Tanganyika. Stanley and Livingstone spent several months together, and Stanley's resulting articles about the horrors of slave trade were published in the New York Herald. They sparked an uproar that resulted several years later in the Sultan of Zanzibar closing his slave market.

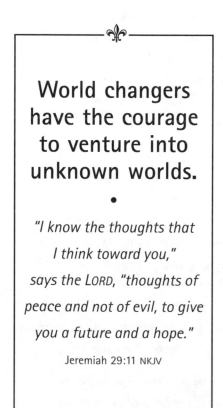

World changers have the courage to venture into unknown worlds.

•

"I know the thoughts that I think toward you," says the LORD, *"thoughts of peace and not of evil, to give you a future and a hope."*

Jeremiah 29:11 NKJV

Although a number of Livingstone's expeditions were considered failures, he was hailed as a hero for having gone to places no white person had ever been, for surviving decades in the harsh environment of Africa, and for doing more than any single person to abolish the African slave trade. He had a worldwide reputation as a geographer, astronomer, ethnologist, anthropologist, chemist, and botanist—he was universally accepted as an expert on central African culture and topography. He was also one of the first missionaries to openly discuss the main reason many Africans did not accept Christianity in the nineteenth century: their concern that Christianity threatened to destroy their native social customs, especially polygamy.[52]

JULIETTE GORDON LOW
(1860–1927)

"She Founded The Girl Scouts"

Everybody called her Daisy. And nobody ever expected her to do what she did.

As a young woman, Georgia-born Daisy spent much of her time giving or attending parties and flitting from one pet project to another. She was charming and entertaining, but those who weren't her friends often thought of her as odd and undependable. She had health problems, could barely hear, and had no children.

But then, at age forty-six, Daisy found herself a restless, lonely widow. She longed to do something worthwhile, even as she slowly returned to her life of parties and travel. Then in May 1911, six years after her husband died, Daisy met the famous British war hero General Sir Robert Baden-Powell at a luncheon. He was the founder of the Boy Scouts, and what Sir Robert told Daisy about his work fascinated her. In March of the next year, she formed two "Girl Guide" patrols. Each girl was given a notebook, pencil, and a yard of cord to practice knot tying. The first name to ever appear under the "Promise" was Daisy's niece and namesake, Margaret "Daisy Doots" Gordon.

By the time the first handbook was published in 1913, the organization's name had officially become "Girl Scouts." Two years later, the first national convention was held, and the following year, Brownies began. Daisy was off to a fast start with her organization.

From the beginning, Daisy sought to give girls more value in their lives, and in turn, she valued the girls in her life. Her first troop outside her home in Scotland was mostly of poor girls who were facing the prospect of leaving home at an early age to work as maids in the city. Daisy developed troop projects to help them earn money raising chickens and spinning wool, which enabled them to stay home with their families. Whenever a problem arose in the Girl Scouts, Daisy's first response was, "Ask the girls. They'll know what's best." This was a radical approach at the time, when few thought children had the ability to make choices.

The Girl Guides took over all of Daisy's thoughts and energy. She paid the organization's expenses the first four years and traveled widely to help interested persons organize new troops. She called on Mrs. Woodrow Wilson, the president's wife, to be the honorary president of the Girl Scouts. Mrs. Wilson accepted, and each subsequent First Lady has been the honorary president of the Girl Scouts. With increasing numbers of troops, and thus increasing costs, Daisy became the organization's principal fund-raiser. One of her favorite ploys was to wear a hat trimmed with parsley and carrots to fashionable lunch-eons. When asked about her hat, she would say, "I can't afford to have this hat done over. I have to save my money for my Girl Scouts. You know about the Girl Scouts, don't you?" At the time of her death, there were nearly 168,000 members of the Girl Scouts. Today, there are more than 3.4 million.[53]

> **World changers are motivated by a desire to do something worthwhile with their lives.**
>
> •
>
> *Don't hide your light! Let it shine for all; let your good deeds glow for all to see, so that they will praise your heavenly Father.*
>
> Matthew 5:15-16 TLB

MARTIN LUTHER
(1483–1546)

"He Launched The Protestant Reformation"

Some people experience success because they are the right people at the right time. In the case of Martin Luther, he seemed to produce the "right words" at the right time—they were words that were to become the sounding gun for the Reformation.

Luther chose to become an Augustinian monk rather than complete his law studies, and in 1512, he received a degree of "Doctor of Theology" from the University of Wittenberg. He later joined its faculty.

Initially Luther was not disenchanted with the Roman Catholic Church. His grievances against the Church rose gradually, as a result of his own spiritual pilgrimage and his studies in the Bible, especially in Paul's letter to the Galatians and to the Romans. In 1510, he took a trip to Rome and was shocked at the worldliness he saw displayed by the clergy. He did not speak out against them, however. Rather, he took aim at the Church's practice of selling indulgences—a granting of remission for certain penalties of sin as the result of giving contributions to the Church. On October 31, 1517—the eve of All Saint's Day—he posted on the door of the Wittenberg church his celebrated *Ninety-five Theses.* In this statement, he strongly denounced corruption in the Church in general and the practice of selling indulgences in particular. Not only were the theses posted on the door, but copies were also distributed widely throughout the area, including a copy to the Archbishop of Mainz.

His protests broadened in scope, and Luther subsequently focused on the limitations of church authority found in the Bible. For this opinion, he was summoned to appear before church officials. After various hearings and orders to recant his position, he was pronounced a heretic and an outlaw. His writings were banned by the Pope.

The outcome for his branding as a heretic would normally have been death by burning at the stake, but Luther's views had found widespread support among the German people, including several German princes. He went into hiding, and his growing support was strong enough to keep him from experiencing any serious criminal penalties imposed by Rome.

As a prolific writer, his works were given mass distribution. His opinion that the Christians should be guided by the Bible and by plain reason was an opinion that gained great popular support. He also translated the Bible into German, which made it possible, of course, for literate people to study the Scriptures themselves. The prose of his Bible translation had a great influence on German language and literature.

Luther advocated that salvation comes only through faith and the grace of God. The doctrine of justification by faith alone gave hope to many who realized like Luther that they could not do enough to save themselves. Finding nothing in the

> **World changers stand up for what they believe and are willing to voice their opinions in the face of danger.**
>
> •
>
> *The mouth of the righteous speaks wisdom, and his tongue talks of justice. The law of his God is in his heart; none of his steps shall slide.*
>
> Psalm 37:30-31 NKJV

Bible to justify the celibacy of clergy, Luther himself married a former nun, and they had six children.

Although Martin Luther was not the first Protestant thinker, he is considered the man chiefly responsible for the Protestant Reformation.[54]

Douglas MacArthur
(1880–1964)

❧

"A Gruff War-Winner With a Compassionate Heart"

General Douglas MacArthur was a military man almost from birth. The son of Lieutenant General Arthur MacArthur, he attended military academies and spent his entire life in military service.

MacArthur led a brigade in World War I and participated in all of the important United States offensives. After the war ended, he was named superintendent of West Point, where he served from 1919 to 1922, and then later was chosen as the U.S. Army chief of staff, a post he held from 1930 to 1935.

MacArthur retired from the army in 1937 to work in the Philippines, with little thought that some of his greatest work still lay ahead. He was in the Philippines when World War II began, and he was recalled to active duty in 1941. He escaped the Japanese invasion of Pearl Harbor, and as U.S. Pacific Commander, he immediately mounted an island-hopping assault that led to the Japanese defeat. He later was named the Commander of the Allied Forces in the Southwest Pacific.

In 1942, under presidential order to move to Australia when it seemed apparent the Philippines would fall to Japan, MacArthur made his famous statement of determination: "I came through, and I shall return." MacArthur waded ashore in the Philippines with his troops in October 1944, fulfilling his promise. By January, his army had recaptured Luzon, the main island of the Philippines, and the next month, had recaptured Manila and Corregidor. It eventually was MacArthur who received the Japanese surrender and directed the occupation of Japan after the war.

During the U.S. campaign to rebuild Japan, MacArthur realized the soul of the Japanese people had been broken and that Japanese values and belief systems were discredited by the war effort. MacArthur's response was to issue a worldwide call for missionaries to bring the Gospel to Japan to help heal the people's broken spirit. MacArthur refused to equate a necessary defeat of a people militarily with a goal to defeat them morally or spiritually. He was a key figure in instilling land reform, restoring the nation's shattered industry, and making Japan more democratic.

At age seventy, General MacArthur was called upon yet again to command the United Nations troops when North Korea attacked South Korea. His career ended for the second time in 1951, when he openly disagreed with U.S. policy to divide Korea and to leave the Communist Chinese in authority over North Korea.

❖

World changers seek peace and restoration, not revenge.

•

I know that the Lord will maintain the cause of the afflicted.

Psalm 140:12 NASB

In addressing a joint session of Congress in April 1951, he closed his speech with a line from an old army ballad: "Old soldiers never die; they just fade away." MacArthur, however, did not fade away. He became a leading figure in Republican politics and was considered a possible presidential candidate in 1952. The nomination, however, went to his former aide, Dwight D. Eisenhower, whose command in Europe during World War II paralleled MacArthur's in the Pacific.[55]

NELSON MANDELA
(1918)

⚜

"A Major Force In Dismantling Apartheid"

Nelson Mandela was born to leadership, but not necessarily the leadership that many expected.

"Rolihlahla" was the tribal name given to Nelson Mandela at his birth. His father was a poor but respected chief of the Tembu, a black African group in southeastern South Africa. Dying, the elder Mandela called the paramount chief of the tribe to his bedside and asked him to raise Rolihlahla, saying, "I can say from the way he speaks to his sisters and friends that his inclination is to help the nation."

The tribal chief sent Mandela to a Christian high school, and he later enrolled in University College at Fort Hare, one of a few colleges that accepted black students. During his third year of college, school authorities took away all powers of the Students' Representative Council, of which Mandela was a member. He protested and was suspended. The chief decided it was time for Mandela to settle down and get married, and Mandela responded by running away to Johannesburg. There, for the first time in his life, he saw the ugliness of segregation and discovered what it meant to be a second-class citizen. Mandela made a decision that he would help his people struggle for freedom and human dignity. He finished college, pursued a law degree, married, and became a member of the African National

Congress. He was also instrumental in founding the Congress Youth League to end discrimination throughout South Africa.

In 1948, the Afrikaner National Party came into power, and the all-white government passed laws of apartheid (separate development for the white and black races). Mandela and other Youth League members protested the imposed curfew for blacks, and he was arrested, the first arrest of what was to become twenty-seven years of off-and-on imprisonment. In the beginning, Mandela's efforts were geared toward nonviolent protest, but as protesters began to be shot by police, he and other black leaders formed "Spear of the Nation," a military wing of the ANC.

In 1964, Mandela was sentenced to life imprisonment on charges of attempting to overthrow the government. He said to the court, "During my lifetime, I have dedicated myself to the struggle of the African people. I have fought against white domination, and I have fought against black domination. I have cherished the ideal of a democratic and free society in which all persons live together in harmony and with equal opportunities. It is an ideal which I hope to live for and to achieve. But if needs be, it is an ideal for which I am prepared to die."

In December 1990, the Prime Minister of South Africa declared "apartheid cannot succeed," and two months later, he announced Mandela's release from prison. Throughout his years in prison,

---

World changers are willing to fight and die for the cause of personal ideals.

•

We know love by this, that He laid down His life for us; and we ought to lay down out lives for the brethren.

1 John 3:16 NASB

Mandela had fought to maintain his dignity and his health. After his release, he renounced all use of violence for political aims, and for four years, he worked with the prime minister, F. W. de Klerk, to bring about a democratic South Africa. In 1994, the boy who had been born a prince, who as a young man became a politician and then a prisoner, was elected president of South Africa in the nation's first open election.[56]

WILL AND CHARLES MAYO
(1861-1939) and (1865-1939)

⚜

"A New Kind Of Medical Clinic"

When Will returned home after completing medical school, a family friend assumed he would work in his father's practice awhile and then move on. "St. Paul or Chicago?" he asked.

Will replied, "To neither one, sir. I intend to remain right here in Rochester and become the greatest surgeon in the world."

A physician and surgeon, Will's father pioneered ovariotomies (removing ovarian tumors). Will and his brother Charles had grown up mixing salves and helping apply bandages and splints. It seemed only natural to them to follow in their father's footsteps. Will went to medical school at age nineteen and Charles at age twenty. They purposefully chose different schools so they might get different viewpoints on medicine. Will specialized in eye surgery.

Then in 1883, Mother Alfred, mother superior of the Sisters of St. Francis, decided to build St. Mary's Hospital in Rochester. It opened in 1889, with forty-five beds, and the Mayos were the primary physicians, not only responsible for medical practice and policy, but also for equipping the operating room. Dr. Charlie built the operating table and made some of the surgical instruments.

Dr. Charlie soon took over the eye surgeries, and Dr. Will specialized in appendectomies. Any time the brothers heard about a new surgical technique, they would travel to see it firsthand—one brother traveling in the spring and the other in the fall to engage in what they termed "brain dusting" by studying with outstanding surgeons. Their singular purpose was to acquire new knowledge, better techniques, and more skill. Along the way, Dr. Charlie continued to invent or improve equipment and instruments to improve surgical treatments of bones, joints, veins, and nerves. Dr. Will added stomach surgery to his expertise and Dr. Charlie, thyroid surgery.

The brothers eventually formed a group they called the Surgeons Club. They invited surgeons to come to Rochester to watch their surgeries, during which they talked nonstop about what they were doing and why. Their reputation began to spread among referring physicians and surgeons, and patients began to travel to Rochester from across the nation. As other surgeons began to move to Rochester to work with them, the Mayos innovated methods for joint consultation about patients, a sharing of patient files, and even in-house conference phone calls—all of which used techniques not seen before in clinics or hospitals. As physicians joined them, they became full "partners" and were given autonomy to travel and study just as the Mayo brothers continued to do. The Mayo Clinic became the first of its kind: a private-practice cooperative group clinic. They also funded the Mayo Foundation for Medical Education and Research to help ensure that Minnesota would be able to provide graduate training in medical specialties long after their deaths.

World changers never think they know it all or think that they must do anything heroic all by themselves.

•

Two can accomplish more than twice as much as one, for the results can be much better.

Ecclesiastes 4:9 TLB

The Mayo brothers literally changed not only the way surgeons shared skills and information, but also the way private medical practice was run—and in the process, they created one of the most highly respected medical centers in the world.[57]

OSEOLA MCCARTY
(1908-1999)

❦

"She Lived A Peaceful, Productive Life And Gave Her All"

At age eight, Oseola McCarty began to work after school with her mother, grandmother, and aunt cleaning clothes brought to their modest Hattiesburg, Mississippi home. It was a job she took on full-time at age twelve when her aunt became too ill to work. It was a job she would continue to do for more than seventy years until arthritis forced her to retire at age eighty-six. Along the way, she nursed her mother, grandmother, and aunt until their deaths.

She led a prayerful, frugal life of solitude, never marrying, never having children, and never learning to drive a car. The boiling water in a cast-iron pot, an old-fashioned rub board, an outdoor "drying line," and crisply starched and ironed clothes were the hallmarks of her world. And once a week, after being paid mostly in one-dollar bills and change, she walked downtown to deposit part of her earnings in a bank savings account.

Oseola never complained about her life. She regarded her work as a blessing since many people in her region of Mississippi did not have jobs. Work and church were her life.

After her retirement, Oseola did something that amazed everyone who knew her, and nearly everyone who would come to hear her story: she turned her life savings—which had grown to $150,000—into an irrevocable trust assigned to the University of Southern Mississippi to provide scholarships for needy students. Her act inspired a capital fund campaign that raised an additional $350,000 for "Oseola McCarty Scholarships." In her words, "Grown-ups can do for themselves. I wanted to give this gift to the children." She refused the university's offer to name a building or create a statue in her honor. She said she would rather attend the graduation of a student who made it through college because of her gift. A foundation executive at the college said, "This is the first time I've experienced anything like this from an individual who simply was not affluent, did not have the resources, and yet gave substantially. . . . She is the most unselfish individual I have ever met."

Her act of giving brought McCarty a great deal of notoriety, including national television appearances, the Presidential Citizens Medal, the Wallenberg Humanitarian Award, and the Avicenna Medal from UNESCO. But fame did not change her, and she refused offers from those who wanted to give her a more prosperous life. "I live where I want to live, and I live the way I want to live," she said.

She and Ted Turner, founder of CNN, once shared a stage in Atlanta. Turner, who had recently given a billion dollars to the United Nations, said, "I admire Oseola McCarty. She gave away her entire life savings. She did more than I did. I just gave away one third—I've still got about $2 billion left. She's the one who really deserves the credit."

In Oseola's words, "I think the way we live matters, not just for now but for always. There is an eternal side to everything you do."[58]

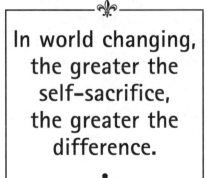

In world changing, the greater the self-sacrifice, the greater the difference.

•

He called his disciples to him and remarked, "That poor widow has given more than all those rich men put together! For they gave a little of their extra fat, while she gave up her last penny."

Mark 12:43-44 TLB

FELIX MENDELSSOHN
(1809–1847)

"A Happy And Fulfilling Life"

Not all people who make a difference have lives marked by tragedy or loss. There are those whose lives are worth emulating for the goodness, wholesomeness, and joy they experienced and imparted. Felix Mendelssohn was such a person. It seems fitting that his very name, Felix, means "happy man" in Latin.

Mendelssohn was encouraged from an early age to develop his musical talent, and although he was required to practice long hours, he also was given abundant time for childhood play. He grew up in a home filled with love, music, and culture. He thoroughly enjoyed dancing, playing billiards and chess, riding horseback, and swimming.

He knew success at an early age and remained successful his entire life. By the time he was nine he was performing publicly, and in his twelfth year, he wrote several symphonies, fugues for string quartet, two operas, and a library of smaller works. As a boy, he became a close friend of Goethe, who once wrote to him, "I am Saul, and you are David. Come to me when I am sad and discouraged and quiet my soul with your sweet harmonies."

The overture to *A Midsummer Night's Dream* was Mendelssohn's first internationally acclaimed work. He also achieved international renown for *Elijah*. It was after a visit to a cave on Staffa Island, one of the Hebrides off Scotland, that Mendelssohn wrote *Fingal's Cave*. The cavern is believed to be the only cavern in the world in which musical sounds are heard as the wind moves through the its prism-shaped pillars.

The first goal Mendelssohn had was to rescue the music of Johann Sebastian Bach from oblivion, which was its state by the time Mendelssohn reached manhood. He reintroduced *Bach's Passion* According to St. Matthew in a special choral concert, and the performance began something of a Bach revival. Mendelssohn said after the 1829 performance of the *Passion* in Berlin, "Everyone was filled with the most solemn devotion."

His second goal was to establish a great music conservatory. After stints as musical director at Dusseldorf, the Gewandhaus Orchestra in Leipzig, and an appointment at the Academy of Arts in Berlin, Mendelssohn made an appeal to the King of Saxony for a conservatory in Leipzig, and he was granted funding for the project in 1843. Mendelssohn shared teaching responsibilities for classes in piano and composition with Robert Schumann and directed the conservatory until his death. He also continued to compose prolifically and to travel often. In all, he made ten trips to England.

> ❧
>
> ## World changers live lives worth imitating.
>
> •
>
> *Give unto the LORD the glory due to His name; Worship the LORD in the beauty of holiness.*
>
> Psalm 29:2 NKJV

By all accounts Mendelssohn married the only woman he had ever loved in 1837 and had an idyllic marriage. In 1847, Mendelssohn received devastating news of his beloved sister's death; he fell unconscious at the report, rupturing a blood vessel in his head. He recovered but remained in ill health, his strength completely dissipated, until his own death several months later.

Mendelssohn's music is marked by elegance and beauty, lyricism and poetry. So, too, his life.[59]

MOSES
About (1500 BCE)

"From Prince To Fugitive To Leader Of A New Nation"

He was hardly a novice young shepherd boy. Rather, Moses was nearly eighty years old when he saw a burning bush in the desert that captured his attention because it was not consumed. He had been tending sheep in the deserts of Moab for nearly forty years.

Not only was the burning bush not consumed, but Moses also heard the voice of God speaking from it. And what God said did not bring Moses joy. When God told Moses that He was going to send him back to Egypt to free the children of Israel, Moses argued, "Who am I, that I should go to Pharaoh?" Moses knew that although he had been rescued from the river by Pharaoh's daughter and had been raised in Pharaoh's court, a new Pharaoh was on the throne, and he, Moses, was a fugitive wanted for murder. Moses also knew that he had little association with the Israelites and that he was slow of speech.

Continuing to argue his inadequacy for the task ahead, Moses was assured of God's presence and His miracle-working power. He promised Moses that Aaron would be his spokesman. Moses asked his father-in-law for permission to return to Egypt with his wife, Zipporah, and their son, and he granted it. And thus, Moses began the third chapter of his life. Repeatedly, Moses went to Pharaoh's court to speak the words of the Lord, "Let My people go."

Amazingly, Moses himself was not killed by the Egyptians as plague after plague erupted in Egypt in the aftermath of Pharaoh's refusals. Amazingly, he was not killed by the Israelites, who experienced an increase in their workload as a result of Pharaoh's anger. The final plague, which brought the death of firstborn children and animals throughout Egypt, moved Pharaoh to grant permission. By that time, the Israelites were also convinced of their need to leave Egypt.

Moses and the people fled only to reach an impasse several days later between the advancing chariots of Pharaoh and the Red Sea. Miraculously, the waters of the sea parted when Moses obeyed the Lord by stretching out his rod over the sea. All of the Israelites walked across the dry sea bottom to safety, but Pharaoh's army and chariots were consumed by the waters of the sea as they attempted to pursue the Israelites.

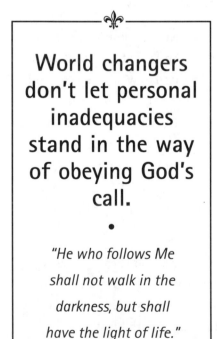

World changers don't let personal inadequacies stand in the way of obeying God's call.

•

"He who follows Me shall not walk in the darkness, but shall have the light of life."

John 8:12 NASB

For forty years, Moses led the Israelites through the wilderness. During those years, Moses interceded often for the Israelites, provided food and water for them as he followed God's directives regarding provision, developed a judicial system for the people, and received from the Lord the commandments that were to provide both the religious laws and social customs for the Israelites.

Throughout Jewish history, Moses has been regarded with high honor as the premier lawgiver and prophet of the Jewish people. The "law" which he gave to the Jewish people at God's command is not only the basis for Jewish law, but it is also at the heart of the judicial systems in England and the United States. The "Ten Commandments" are regarded by millions of people as being the core of morality for more than 4,000 years.[60]

John Muir
(1838–1914)

❧

"Guardian Of The Wilderness"

John Muir immigrated to the United States with his family when he was ten years old and spent his teen years on the family's farm in Wisconsin, enjoying every hour he could escape to the nearby woods. In the winters, he spent his time inventing a sawmill, water wheels, thermometers, clocks, and other devices.

His inventions led him to enroll in the university, where he became fascinated with botany and began to keep a journal of his travels and nature studies. He hiked and camped extensively through Wisconsin, Indiana, and Ontario, Canada, and he completed a 1,000-mile walk across the southeastern United States. At age thirty, he traveled to San Francisco in search of "anywhere that is wild."

His search ended in Yosemite Valley, which became his home, classroom, and laboratory. It was while climbing and studying the mountains and glaciers of Yosemite—his "University of the Wilderness"—that Muir learned about the damage the grazing sheep were doing to the mountain environment. He also became alarmed that the huge, ancient sequoia trees were being cut for lumber.

In the winter months Muir worked as a sawyer, and in the springs and summers, he guided tourists through Yosemite. He also tramped the wildernesses of Nevada, Utah, California, the Pacific Northwest, and Alaska. At age forty-two, he married Louise Stentzel, and for eight years, he spent much of his time running the Stentzel fruit ranch, with periodic excursions to Alaska and especially to Glacier Bay.

As the result of articles he wrote about his travels and wilderness studies, he gained a reputation as the "guardian of the wilderness." He combined scientific information with narratives of his outdoor adventures, including several brushes with death. His fame grew, and he spent increasing amounts of time in the San Francisco area to be near research libraries. He noted, "They will see what I meant in time. There must be places for human beings to satisfy their souls. Food and drink is not all. There is the spiritual."

Muir's family leased or sold part of the Stentzel ranch so he could work full-time writing and defending wilderness areas. In the early 1880s, he began work on national legislation to enlarge the government-protected areas in Yosemite Valley and nearby Mariposa Big Tree Grove; and to set aside land in the Sierra Nevada as a public park. He spoke often about the forests being "God's first temples." His work led to the creation of Yosemite, Sequoia, and Kings Canyon national parks in California.

In 1892, friends of Muir formed the Sierra Club and elected Muir its president. He later joined the national Forestry Commission in Chicago, which recommended to

> ❧
> # World changers often admire and preserve God's creation.
>
> •
>
> *Do you know the time the mountain goats give birth?*
> *Do you observe the calving of the deer?*
> *Can you count the men this they fulfill,*
> *Or do you know the time they give birth? . . .*
> *Who sent out the wild donkey free?*
> *And who loosed the bonds of the swift donkey?*
>
> Job 39:1-2,5 NASB

President Cleveland that thirteen new nature preserves be established in eight states, that timber and mining laws be changed to eliminate "fraud and robbery," and that the Grand Canyon and Mount Rainier be named national parks. He later urged President Theodore Roosevelt to establish the Forest Service. He was considered the strongest voice of the "conservation movement" and has been called the "father of our national parks."[61]

SIR ISAAC NEWTON
(1642–1727)

⚜

"The Most Influential Scientist Who Ever Lived"

Isaac Newton was born in England on Christmas Day—a day known for giving presents—and in many ways, his life was a present to mankind. Very little in the way that people lived day-to-day life had changed in the 500 years prior to Newton. However, virtually everything changed in the 500 years after—people's dress, foods, work, and leisure pursuits. The discoveries made possible by Newton's theories and laws impacted the full range of human experience.

As a child, the young Isaac showed mechanical aptitude, and he was clever with his hands. He was bored, however, with school, and he failed in geometry because he didn't do his problems "according to the book." When he was a teenager, his mother took him out of school in hopes he might become at least a successful farmer. At eighteen, she finally gave in to the suggestions of others that he enter Cambridge University, and there, Newton very quickly showed great interest and ability in science and mathematics. He soon moved out into areas of original research. It was between the ages of twenty-one and twenty-seven that he laid the foundation for the scientific theories that subsequently revolutionized the world.

The first of Newton's discoveries to be published was his ground-breaking work on the nature of light. He discovered that ordinary white light is a mixture of all the colors of the rainbow. Using the laws of reflection and refraction of light, he designed and built the first reflecting telescope in 1668. He invented the concept of integral calculus when he was in his early twenties. This invention formed the basis for modern mathematical theory and is the foundation for much of the progress of modern science. He also discovered the second, third, and fourth laws of motion, which taken together with Galileo's first law of motion, created a unified system by which virtually all mechanical systems are devised—from the swinging of a pendulum to the motion of the planets in orbits around the sun. His innovative laws and their applications radically changed the field of astronomy.

More scientists have given reference to Newton and to his laws and discoveries than to any other individual scientist. Not all of his contemporaries were fans of his, however. Voltaire sharply criticized Newton for stating that Daniel 12:4 might mean that human beings would eventually develop a system of transportation that would enable a person to travel at a speed of fifty miles per hour.

Although he believed strongly in the validity and applicability of his own work, Newton was a very humble man and was reluctant to publish his results. Many of his theories were not public until long after he developed them and then only because a colleague insisted. He once said, "I can take my telescope and look millions and millions of miles into space, but I can lay it aside and go into my room, shut the door, get down on my knees in earnest prayer, and see more of Heaven and get closer to God than I can assisted by all the telescopes and material agencies on earth."

Newton was the first scientist ever to be buried in Westminster Abbey as a national hero.[62]

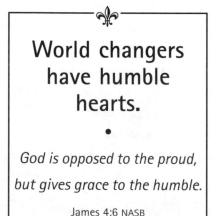

World changers have humble hearts.

•

God is opposed to the proud, but gives grace to the humble.

James 4:6 NASB

FLORENCE NIGHTINGALE
(1820–1910)

❧

"She Made Nursing A Genuine Profession"

Every summer the Nightingale family traveled to their home in Derbyshire, and on her walks around the area, Florence found herself drawn to the nearby cottages and their extremely poor inhabitants. She felt great personal satisfaction in taking them food, clothes, and medicine. She had those same feelings of purpose as she cared for an orphaned baby, nursed her grandmother through a serious illness, and spent the final minutes of her nanny's life at her bedside. She concluded that God had called her to care for the sick.

Florence wasn't content, however, with offering hot drinks or smoothing pillows. She wanted to study the best ways to help patients, to assist with surgery, and to handle birth and death confidently. She sought out a place for training. Her family was appalled at her decision since nurses had a reputation at that time of being drunken, careless, and dirty; and Victorian hospitals had a reputation for being places of disease more than health. So, Florence began her pursuit of nursing in secret. By day, she lived a passive well-to-do life. At night, she studied hospital reports and wrote letters to request information about health-care in Europe. She did this for sixteen years—a period about which she said, "I went down into the depths." During those years, she managed only to train briefly as a nurse in Germany.

Then, at age thirty-three, still battling strong objections from her family, she accepted the job of Superintendent of London's Institution for the Care of Sick Gentlewomen in Distressed Circumstances. In ten days, she took over a new location and made it ready for patients. The hospital directors and staff members were astonished—they had expected changes, but they hadn't counted on Florence to move so quickly. Her years of study had showed her what could and must be done. Her long endurance had also taught her not to take "no" for an answer.

She began a one-woman campaign to rid the hospital of all filth and to make nursing an honorable profession. She personally spent countless hours at the bedside of patients. The hospital became a well-publicized success. When Sidney Herbert, the Secretary of State for War, asked Florence to take a party of British nurses to the hospital barracks near the Crimean War front, she quickly mobilized thirty-eight nurses. Known among the soldiers as the "Lady with the Lamp," she worked around the clock and eventually became seriously ill herself. Queen Victoria wrote in admiration of her efforts: "I wish she were at the War Office."

Florence returned to England in 1856, and for the next fifty years, she rarely left her sickbed but nevertheless, changed the face of nursing. She wrote a thousand-page document titled Notes on Matters Affecting the Health, Efficiency and Hospital Administration of the British Army, set up and supervised a school for nurses, worked on reform laws that impacted nursing and childbirth, and campaigned for good ventilation and good drainage. Even when she went blind at age eighty-one, she maintained lively contact with the nurses at the Nightingale School.[63]

> ❧
>
> ## World changers are persistent in their pursuit of those things they know are God's desire.
>
> •
>
> *The work of the godly will flourish.*
>
> Proverbs 14:11 TLB

Jesse Owens
(1913–1980)

✤

"He Calmly 'Flew' In The Face Of Prejudice"

No stranger to racial prejudice, Jesse Owens grew up in a small town in the South, the son of a sharecropper, at a time when blacks had no rights, no legal protection, and few educational opportunities. By the time he moved to Cleveland, Ohio, he was so conciliatory to the white majority around him that he allowed a teacher to rename him Jesse—she had mistakenly thought he was saying "Jesse" when he was actually saying "J. C." (the initials of his name, James Cleveland, and the name he went by in the South).

As a child, Jesse Owens was frail, shy, and sickly. It was a teacher who speculated that sports might help improve his health. Running became his favorite activity, in part because Owens later noted, "We couldn't afford any kind of equipment, and we had nothing to do but run." And so Jesse, in his own words, "ran and ran and ran." He later said, "I loved [running] because it was something you could do all by yourself, and under your own power."

Owen's first official race was a losing effort in a 40-yard dash. He said, "I got left in the holes," referring to the holes that sprinters dug in an era before starting blocks. The loss only made Owens more determined to run faster. By the time he was a senior in high school, he was setting high-school world records. He attended Ohio State University at a time before college scholarships were given to track-and-field athletes, and he operated a night elevator at the State Office Building so that he could run by day.

In a fall in 1935, just days before the Big Ten meet, Owens was seriously injured. On the day of the meet, he was in such pain that he was unable to warm up. He chose to concentrate on the one thing that mattered to him more than pain: competing. He hurdled, dashed, and broad-jumped his way to five world records and tied for a sixth in less than an hour. His one jump in the long jump established a world record that stood for a quarter of a century, longer than any other track-and-field mark has ever stood.

The 1936 Olympics were held in Berlin and were intended to be used by Nazi leader Adolph Hitler as a demonstration of the supremacy of the white race. His intended demonstration of an Aryan-supremacy theory was demolished by the stunning performances of a number of American blacks, whom Hitler had ridiculed as "black auxiliaries." The most notable performance was that of Owens, who won four gold medals. In just six days, Owens broke Olympic records nine times and tied them twice. He won gold in the 100-meter race, broad jump, 200-meter dash, and as part of the 400-meter relay team. The 100,000 fans who saw him perform were at first struck to silence by his performance but then hailed him as the supreme athlete in the world. A street in Berlin was named for him.

> **World changers don't listen to the hisses of others but respond to the quiet call of success within.**
>
> •
>
> *A man's wisdom gives him patience; it is to his glory to overlook an offense.*
>
> Proverbs 19:11

A long-time stutterer, Owens overcame his speech difficulties to give as many as 200 inspirational speeches during the last twenty years of his life. His hometown engraved a monument in his honor: "He inspired a world enslaved in tyranny and brought hope to his fellow man."[64]

ROSA PARKS
(1913)

❧

"The Mother Of The Modern-Day Civil Rights Movement"

Rosa Louise Parks is someone few would have marked to become a hero. Born in Tuskegee, Alabama, she was educated in a rural schoolhouse and completed her education at age eleven. Her mother then enrolled her in Montgomery Industrial School for Girls (also known as Miss White's School for Girls), and several years later, she went to Alabama State Teachers' College for Negroes for tenth and eleventh grade. She was unable to graduate with her class, however, because of illness and the death of her grandmother. As she prepared to return to school, her mother became ill, and Rosa remained at home to care for her. It wasn't until 1934, at the age of twenty-one that she received her high school diploma.

Serving as secretary and later, as youth leader of the Montgomery branch National Association for the Advancement of Colored People (NAACP), Rosa worked with her husband Raymond. She was preparing for a major NAACP youth conference at the time she took a bold action that changed not only her life, but also the life of the nation.

Rosa has said, "As a child, I learned from the Bible to trust in God and not be afraid. I have always felt comforted by reading the Psalms, especially Psalms 23 and 27. . . . I felt the Lord would give me the strength to endure whatever I had to face. God did away with all my fear. It was time for someone to stand up—or in my case, sit down. I refused to move."

While riding a city bus on December 1, 1955, Rosa refused to surrender her seat to a white male passenger. Her quiet act of protest resulted in her arrest and a fine of ten dollars plus court costs. Her arrest also sparked a boycott of the city bus line by the black people of Montgomery and sympathizers of civil rights for blacks. For 381 days, blacks who had used the city buses either walked or arranged other transportation in the city. The events in Montgomery set in motion a chain of events that included nonviolent sit-ins, eat-ins, swim-ins, and walk-outs in other parts of the nation. The bus boycott in Montgomery ended on December 21, 1956, after the United States Supreme Court declared bus segregation unconstitutional. The day after the boycott ended, Rosa rode a nonsegregated bus for the first time. She later said, "It is funny to me how people came to believe that the reason that I did not move from my seat was that my feet were tired. . . . My feet were not tired, but I was tired—tired of unfair treatment."

Rosa and her husband moved to Detroit in 1957, but they remained active in the civil rights movement, traveling, speaking, and participating in peaceful demonstrations. From 1965 to 1988, Rosa worked in the office of Congressman John Conyers of Michigan. In 1987, she began the Rosa and Raymond Parks Institute for Self-Development, an organization designed to motivate and direct youth to achieve their highest potential. She has spoken

> # World changers often resist evil in peaceful ways.
>
> •
>
> *Humble yourselves under the mighty hand of God, that He may exalt you in due time.*
>
> 1 Peter 5:6 NKJV

extensively at schools, colleges, and national organizations on the theme of human potential and the freedom necessary to pursue potential. Says Rosa, "As long as people use tactics to oppress or restrict other people from being free, there is work to be done."[65]

LOUIS PASTEUR

(1822-1895)

⚜

"His Worked Saved And Extended The Lives Of Countless Millions"

As a chemistry student in college, Louis Pasteur was called mediocre by his professors. But Pasteur didn't let the opinion of professors influence him. By age twenty-six, Pasteur had completed a doctorate degree, conducted research on the mirror-image isomers of tartaric acid, and was a renowned chemist.

It was when Pasteur turned his attention to the study of fermentation that he began the work for which he became most famous. He demonstrated that the presence of certain species of microorganisms could produce undesirable products in the fermenting of beverages, and this led him to conclude that some species of microorganisms might produce undesirable products and effects in human beings. He became an ardent champion of "the germ theory of disease" and embarked on a campaign to stress antiseptic methods for physicians and surgeons. He developed a technique for destroying microorganisms in beverages, including milk—"pasteurization"—a technique that subsequently saved millions of children's lives.

Pasteur also saved entire industries. His studies and conclusions related to fermentation resulted in changes being made to improve the state-operated brewing, distilling, and wine-making industries in France. The financial benefits were enough for France to pay the huge indemnity it incurred in the Franco-German War. He also saved the silk industry of France by discovering the parasite that caused silkworm disease.

In his mid-fifties, Pasteur turned his attention to a study of anthrax, a serious infectious disease that attacked cattle, other animals, and human beings. He was able to isolate a particular species of bacterium responsible for the disease, but more importantly, he developed a technique for producing a weakened strain of the anthrax bacillus. When injected into cattle, this weakened strain produced a mild but not fatal form of the disease. The result was cattle with greater immunity to anthrax. In essence, he had created a "vaccine."

The foundation for isolating the germs of tuberculosis, cholera, diphtheria, lockjaw, and a number of other infectious diseases, Pasteur also laid. Pasteur's most renowned single achievement was developing a technique for inoculating people against rabies. Other scientists, applying his basic ideas, developed vaccines against other serious diseases, including epidemic typhus and poliomyelitis. Since Pasteur's time, life expectancies in much of the world have nearly doubled. Most scientists consider this enormous increase in human life spans and consequently, human productivity and

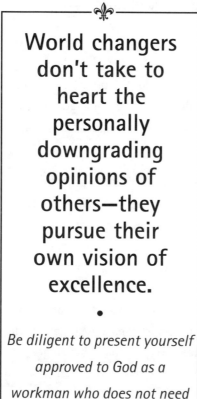

World changers don't take to heart the personally downgrading opinions of others—they pursue their own vision of excellence.

•

Be diligent to present yourself approved to God as a workman who does not need to be ashamed, accurately handling the word of truth.

2 Timothy 2:15 NASB

quality of life, to be the direct result of Pasteur's work in germ theory and the development of vaccines. He is considered by many to be the most important single figure in the history of medicine.

The Pasteur Institute, which was founded in his honor and led by him from 1888 until his death, continues internationally recognized research in bacteriology to this day.[66]

St. Patrick
(385 est.–461)

"He Brought 'Light' To Ireland"

The first time Patrick went to Ireland, it was not by choice. When he was only sixteen, he and a number of other youth were kidnapped and sold into slavery in pagan Ireland.

Patrick spent six years pasturing flocks, enduring extreme hardships. He later wrote in his book, *Confession,* that at sixteen, he "knew not the true God," but in Ireland, Patrick began to pray. He wrote, "The love and fear of God more and more inflamed my heart; my faith enlarged, my spirit grew. . . . I said a hundred prayers by day and almost as many by night. I arose before day in the snow, in the frost, and the rain, yet I received no harm . . . for then the spirit of God was within me."

In a dream, Patrick heard a voice saying he was soon to be free. He took that as a sign to make an escape, and he ran 200 miles to the sea. After gaining passage on a ship and sailing three days, Patrick and the others on board traveled for twenty-eight days more on foot through unknown countryside until their provisions ran out. Patrick encouraged the sailors to trust God to provide for them, and almost immediately, a herd of wild pigs crossed their path. They killed a number of them, ate their fill, offered thanks to God, and at length, reached habitation. At age twenty-three, Patrick was restored to his family.

And then came the call. One night he heard Irish voices calling him back to Ireland, saying, "We beg you, holy youth, to come and walk among us again." Patrick answered this call, leaving his family voluntarily this time and resuming his education. He studied for the priesthood and was ordained in 417. He worked as a priest in Auxerre, France, for about fifteen years, always with a desire to minister in Ireland, and in 432, St. Germanus consecrated him bishop and sent him to Ireland.

Soon after his arrival, Patrick lit a bonfire on the eve of Easter. The local king had ordered that no fires be lighted that night until the court druids had lit their fires for a sacred druid festival. Seeing Patrick's blaze in the distance, the High King Laoghaire ordered Patrick to his court for punishment. The king, queen, and courtiers were so struck by the nobility of Patrick's bearing that they gave him an opportunity to speak. He said of the druids, "They can bring darkness, but they cannot bring Light." He preached Christ to the court and made converts of the queen and her two daughters, as well as some of the druids present. He was released unharmed.

For the next twenty-five years, Patrick worked tirelessly in Ireland, facing great perils and hardships. He fasted often, prayed nearly continuously, built churches and monasteries, ordained priests and bishops, baptized and confirmed new believers, and gave Ireland a new faith. When he died, Ireland as a nation mourned him for twelve days.

He said of his work in Ireland, "I am ready to give my life most willingly; to spend myself even to death in this country. . . . Among

> **Those who spend their lives in service to Christ are always world changers in God's eyes.**
>
> •
>
> *I have directed you in the way of wisdom; I have led you in upright paths.*
>
> Proverbs 4:11 NASB

this people I want to wait for the promise made by Christ in the Gospel, 'They shall come from the east and the west, and sit down with Abraham, Isaac, and Jacob.'"[67]

ST. PAUL
(2–65 estimated)

❧

"Apostle To The Gentiles"

Paul, whose original name was Saul, was of the tribe of Benjamin, born in Tarsus. He was brought up as a Pharisee and educated at Jerusalem under the celebrated Rabbi Gamaliel. He spoke Greek and Syro-Chaldaic (Hebrew), had tent-making as his trade, and was a Roman citizen.

As a zealous young Pharisee, he spoke against Christianity and consented to the martyrdom of Stephen. He obtained orders from the high priest to travel to Damascus to persecute the Christians there. As he neared Damascus, a miraculous light blinded him and caused him to fall to the earth, trembling with fear. He heard the voice of Jesus directing him to go into the city to learn what he should do. He was led blind into Damascus and remained in that state until Ananias, also sent by the Lord, came to him, restored his sight, and baptized him.

Once converted, Paul went to Arabia for a while, then returned to Damascus and began to preach the Gospel. His enthusiasm for Jesus Christ amazed those who heard him. He escaped from Damascus after learning of a plot to take his life and went to Jerusalem, where the Christians there became convinced of his conversion and received him. He moved to Tarsus shortly after and joined forces with Barnabas. Together, they went to Antioch, where they established its first

Gentile church. They soon were sent by the Antioch church on a mission into Judea, and later, as missionaries to Seleucia, Cyprus, Paphos, Perga, Antioch in Pisidia, Iconium, Lystra, Derbe, and Attalia. After a four-year period back in Antioch, Paul attended a church council at Jerusalem, and the following year, he embarked on his second missionary journey, this time accompanied by Timothy and Luke. He went into Macedonia and preached at Philippi, Thessalonica, Beroea, Athens, Corinth, and Ephesus.

After a short rest, he began his third trip, this time spending two years teaching in Ephesus and traveling through Macedonia and Greece. The trip ended in Jerusalem, where he was seized and cast out of the temple on an erroneous charge of bringing a Gentile into a forbidden area. Paul was arraigned before the Sanhedrin but appealed to Rome for trial. After years of imprisonment in Caesarea, he was sent to Rome, where he continued to preach while under house arrest. Tradition holds that he was beheaded in 65 A.D. by Nero. During his life, he wrote at least thirteen epistles covering virtually all matters of Christian faith.

❦

World changers are willing to help just one person.

•

I have set you as a light to the Gentiles, that you should be for salvation to the ends of the earth.

Acts 13:47 NKJV

Throughout his travels, Paul wrote that he had been lashed, beaten, stoned, shipwrecked, and was often in peril, weary, hungry, thirsty, cold, and naked (see 2 Corinthians 11:23-28). He said, however, "I take pleasure in . . . distresses, for Christ's sake. For when I am weak, then I am strong" (2 Corinthians 12:10 NKJV).

Paul was a hero to many in the early Christian church, but perhaps no more so than to those who experienced miracles at his hand. One such person was a young slave girl in Philippi who was possessed by a spirit of divination and was used by her masters for fortune-telling. Paul said to the spirit, "I command you in the name of Jesus Christ to come out of her." To her, Paul no doubt was the greatest hero on earth.[68]

J. C. PENNEY
(1875–1971)

❧

"He Built A Financial Empire On The Golden Rule"

When James Cash Penney's father told him that he would have to start buying his own clothing, the eight-year-old boy acted quickly. He ran errands, sold junk, and invested in a pig. He soon had purchased a dozen pigs . . . but then the neighbors began to complain. His father called a halt to the enterprise, saying, "We can't take advantage of our neighbors." His words became part of Penney's lifelong business philosophy.

After high school Penney clerked in a store and then moved to Colorado, where he opened a butcher shop. That venture failed when he refused to supply a bottle of bourbon each week to the chef of a local hotel. The owner of a Wyoming dry goods store gave Penney his next chance by helping him open his own store in Kemmerer. Penney called it "The Golden Rule Store." Five years later, he added two more stores and introduced profit-sharing for his employees.

By 1912, he owned thirty-four stores. Two years later, he incorporated and moved his headquarters to New York City. By 1917, at age thirty-nine, he resigned as president and became Chairman of the Board. During the next twelve years, the chain of stores grew to 1,400 stores nationwide.

Along the way Penney's personal life was marked by tragedy. His first wife died in 1910, and then his second wife died in childbirth in

1923. He said later that he experienced an intense desire to drink after his first wife's death—a desire that was "persistent and terrible, lasting not only through weeks and months, but even years. Many a night I walked the streets battling with this temptation and the darkness that had settled upon me." He had similar feelings after the stock market crash in 1929, when J. C. Penney stock plunged from 120 points to only thirteen. He was virtually broke by 1932, and he had to drop many of his Christian philanthropies, among them the Christian Herald magazine for which he wrote a popular column for many years. He eventually wound up in a Battle Creek, Michigan sanitarium. While there, he regained his faith and hope. His health and spirit renewed, he began the long climb back to the financial top at the age of fifty-six.

By 1951, there was a J. C. Penney store in every state, and for the first time sales surpassed $1 billion. During the 1950s, Penney expanded the merchandise lines to include major appliances, home electronics, furniture, and sporting goods. The chain added J. C. Penney Financial Services in 1967 and purchased the Thrift Drug Company in 1969. Penney remained the company's premier goodwill ambassador long after retirement. He attended fifty-one store openings, participated in twenty-seven TV and radio programs, gave 105 speeches, and traveled 62,000 miles at age eighty-four!

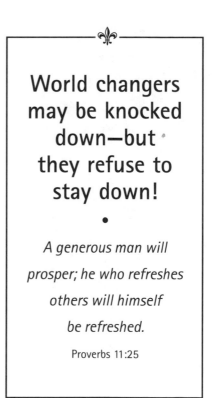

World changers may be knocked down—but they refuse to stay down!

•

A generous man will prosper; he who refreshes others will himself be refreshed.

Proverbs 11:25

The Penney Idea, or code of ethics, was adopted in 1913 and asked the consumer for "a fair remuneration and not all the profit the traffic will bear." The company, in turn, promised to deliver value, quality, and satisfaction. The company promised "to test our every policy, method and act in this wise: 'Does it square with what is right and just?'" Penney stuck by his "Golden Rule" ethic even in hard financial times and even when mocked by peers.[69]

ITZHAK PERLMAN
(1945)

❧

"He Has Never Given Up On His Life's Dream"

There are those who allow life's tragedies to steal their dreams. Itzhak Perlman is not among them.

When he was only three years old, Itzhak sat attentively as he listened to an hour-long violin recital program on the radio. At the program's end, he announced to his mother that he wanted to grow up to be a violinist. His mother bought him a toy violin, and within days, he had learned to play tunes on it.

Itzhak Perlman was born in Israel. At the age of four, he became seriously ill with polio and lost the use of his legs. He quickly adapted, however, to his paralysis. He wore braces and used crutches to continue to attend school. Because he could no longer run and play freely, however, he concentrated on music. His parents bought him a secondhand fiddle for six dollars, and by age five, he was admitted to the Tel Aviv Academy of Music. He practiced relentlessly, and at age ten, he performed his first solo recital, Rimsky-Korsakov's "Flight of the Bumblebee," a piece that demands great precision and speed.

In 1958, Ed Sullivan, who hosted a popular TV variety program in the United States, traveled to Israel in search of new talent. He learned of Itzhak, who was thirteen at the time and considered a child prodigy. Sullivan was struck not only by the boy's talent, but also by his courage and good humor. He invited him to appear on *The Ed Sullivan Show,* which Itzhak did in February 1959. He was an immediate hit with American audiences, and he, in turn, fell in love with the United States. He began to train at the prestigious Juilliard School of Music in New York City.

At age nineteen, Perlman became the youngest competitor to reach the finals of the Leventritt Competition, a contest which had a cash award and led to opportunities for appearances with American symphony orchestras. Perlman borrowed a 200-year-old Guarneri violin from Juilliard's rare instrument competition for the finals at Carnegie Hall . . . and won! At the celebration afterward, the priceless violin was stolen. Perlman was horrified, and for a day, he was devastated more than triumphant. And then, the Guarneri was discovered for sale at a nearby pawnshop—for fifteen dollars.

In New York City noted violinist Isaac Stern and Perlman became friends. Stern liked Perlman's jokes and booming laugh as much as he respected his talent. His association with Stern led to a concert with the New York Philharmonic. The crowd applauded Perlman to five curtain calls. With Stern's endorsement, Perlman toured the United States and then traveled to Europe in the late 1960s. He has never stopped traveling and performing and is considered by many to be the greatest living violinist.

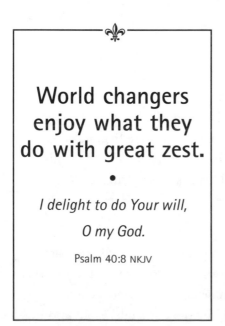

World changers enjoy what they do with great zest.

•

I delight to do Your will,

O my God.

Psalm 40:8 NKJV

Many of those who review Perlman's concerts note one thing: his great love of life. He enjoys playing all kinds of music— ragtime, jazz, and klezmer dance music as well as classical. He was presented the Medal of Freedom in a ceremony at the White House in 1986. His recordings have sold millions of copies worldwide, and he has one of the most recognizable faces in classical music—a face that usually has a smile on it.[70]

RONALD REAGAN
(1911)

❖

"He Presided Over The End Of The Cold War"

Ronald Reagan, 40th President of the United States, is known for his buoyant optimism. It is a trait he appears to have had from child-hood, in spite of the difficulties of growing up in a very modest home and with an alcoholic father, an early bout with viral pneumonia, and numerous accidents and injuries.

At the height of the Great Depression, Reagan graduated from Eureka College, having worked his way through school with a sports scholarship and a job in the kitchen of his fraternity house. After college, he became a radio sportscaster in Davenport, Iowa, providing commentary on more than 600 baseball games. He took up horseback riding and joined a U.S. Army special cavalry unit. In 1937, while in California reporting on a spring training camp, he approached a Hollywood studio for a screen test. He won a contract with Warner Brothers and soon after, appeared in the first of fifty-three films in which he would have a part.

During World War II, Reagan was called into active duty in the U.S. Army and was assigned to narrate Army Air Corps training films. He began to take interest in organizations set up to benefit screen actors and was among the actors who testified in Washington during the McCarthy investigations on behalf of entertainers who were not communists. He became president of the Screen Actors Guild in 1947. In

1954, he became the spokesperson for the General Electric Theater, a weekly television program. He also gave speeches on behalf of G.E. across the nation.

Although he was a Democrat in his early years, Reagan found himself aligning more and more with conservative politics; and in 1962, he voted as a Republican. He actively campaigned and raised funds for the Republican Party in the 1964 presidential campaign; and in 1966, he scored a stunning victory in his bid to be governor of California. During his two terms as governor, he led a move to reform the state's tax, welfare, and education systems; and to turn the state's budget from a deficit to a surplus. In 1975, he "retired" to his ranch and devoted his time to speaking engagements and writing a weekly newspaper column.

Elected president in 1980 with a landslide victory, Reagan immediately moved to enact a major tax cut that turned a sluggish U.S. economy toward prosperity. He led an effort to create a network of weapon interception devices known as "Star Wars" (Strategic Defense Initiative) and held meetings with the leader of the Soviet Union to bring an end to the "cold war" and to initiate the first arms-reduction acts. He developed a strong policy against terrorism and selected the first woman to the Supreme Court.

Reagan survived an assassination attempt and continued for years after his presidency to be one of the nation's most popular and highly-paid speakers and authors, primarily because his message was up-beat, inspirational, and rooted in enduring values.

> ❧
>
> # World changers change things wherever they are.
>
> •
>
> *Blessed is the man to whom the LORD does not impute iniquity, and in whose spirit there is no deceit!*
>
> Psalm 32:2 NASB

What many people don't know about Ronald Reagan is that he worked as a lifeguard for seven summers and is credited with saving seventy-seven people from drowning. In addition to his many political accomplishments, Ronald Reagan is most certainly a hero to those he rescued![71]

PAUL REVERE
(1735–1818)

❧

"His Name Became A Synonym For Patriotism"

Paul Revere was born to Apollos Rivoire, who had immigrated to the new world alone at age thirteen. Rivoire apprenticed to a Boston metalsmith who was a quiet, religious man. By the time he was twenty-eight, he opened his own silver shop. He changed his name to Revere, married; and in 1735, Paul was born. Paul grew up in comfort, and after finishing his formal schooling at age thirteen, he became an apprentice in his father's shop. In his spare time, he and friends formed a "society" to ring the bells of Christ Church, and he listened to the sermons of Jonathan Mayhew, who spoke boldly against the tyranny of kings.

After his father died in 1754, Paul took over responsibility for the silver shop. Two years later, he answered a call to arms to fight French soldiers who were raiding the colonies, and he spent a year as a soldier. He married, fathered six children, and became a master silversmith. When England passed the Stamp Act, he began to meet with others in Boston who took the name Sons of Liberty and had as their rallying cry, "taxation without representation is tyranny." He gained a reputation as a man who could get things done. Silver was a luxury in the colonies, and Revere expanded his trade: he engraved copper plates, became a political cartoonist, and learned to make false teeth. His drawing of a Liberty Tree became a well-known symbol in the colonies. Revere's wife died giving birth to their seventh child, and he remarried; he and his second wife had eight children. In 1773, he did something unusual for a silversmith: he bought a horse and taught himself to ride well.

When the Boston Tea Party took place in December 1773, Revere rode his horse 350 miles in eleven days to New York and Philadelphia to tell what had happened. He made the trip a second time when England blocked the Boston harbor and a third time to deliver the Suffolk Resolves to the first Continental Congress. When not traveling or working, he spied on the British in their taverns. The spying network was effective in discovering the British plans to attack Concord. Paul was one of two riders chosen to spread word of the attack—since he was well-known, he was chosen to go a secret route, across the Charles River in a rowboat and then make the rest of the journey on horseback. It was April 18, 1775, when he made his famous midnight ride. Even though he was pursued by the British, he made his way safely to Lexington to inform Hancock and Adams of the attack.

About halfway to Concord, he was captured by the British but was quickly released.

During the Revolutionary War, Revere learned to make cannons and gunpowder, and he supervised a powder mill. He engraved copper plates for the printing of paper money and the official colonial seal. He rode as an express rider, and for a while, he was commander of the fort at Castle Island. After the war, he made copper sheathing for the Constitution ship and for the dome of the Boston statehouse

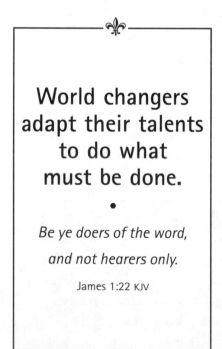

World changers adapt their talents to do what must be done.

•

Be ye doers of the word, and not hearers only.

James 1:22 KJV

and other buildings. He also became an expert bell maker, producing more than 400 bells for churches throughout New England. It seemed fitting that he died on a Sunday because church bells he had made rang all over Boston.[72]

CAL RIPKEN JR.
(1961)

❦

"A Strong Work Ethic"

When did "The Streak" start? On May 30, 1982, when a young player named Cal started for the Orioles against the Blue Jays. He played third, batted eighth, and didn't get a hit. It was an unnoticed "beginning."

If you ask Cal, however, when The Streak began, he is likely to refer to his childhood home, minor-league clubhouses where he worked during the summers, and his father's garage where he sorted nuts and bolts on rainy days. He has said, "My dad has always been driven to do everything the right way and do it to completion. I don't know what kind of effect that has had on The Streak, but I know a work ethic is everything to my dad, and in baseball it's everything to me." The work ethic was passed on to Cal like a torch from father to son.

Today, Cal Ripken Jr. holds the record for the most consecutive games played in a professional baseball career. He eclipsed the record set by Lou Gehrig, the "Iron Horse" of the New York Yankees, from 1925 to 1939. The new record of 2,131 games came on September 6, 1995. Ripken had played every Oriole game for nearly fourteen consecutive years. As icing on the cake, he hit a home run in both the record-tying and tie-breaking games.

In 1978 at the age of seventeen, Cal began to play baseball. After playing at the Orioles' farm and AAA clubs, he joined the parent club in the majors in 1981, at the age of twenty. His father, a former baseball player, manager, and coach, taught him "you can't contribute from the bench;" and from the beginning, Cal has had a desire to play every game, not just show up for it. Cal was fortunate in avoiding injuries—on only two nights in thirteen years did injury threaten to keep him in the dugout. His fellow players claim he just doesn't feel pain, or if he does, he doesn't let it stop him. The Baltimore manager once quipped, "If the good Lord wants him to have an off day, He'll let it rain."

As Cal approached Gehrig's record, he was nearly sidelined by a players' strike and by his own batting slump. He persevered through both.

More than an "endurance man" in baseball, Cal Ripken Jr. is the only player in major league history to start in twelve consecutive All-Star games, and he is the only player to win an MVP Award the year after winning a Rookie of the Year Award. He said after breaking the record, "I stand here, overwhelmed, as my name is linked with the great and courageous Lou Gehrig. I'm truly humbled to have our names spoken in the same breath. Some may think our strongest connection is because we both played many consecutive games. Yet I believe in my heart that our true link is a common motivation—a love of the game of baseball, a passion for our team, and a desire to compete on the very highest level. . . . You are challenged by the game of baseball to do your very best day in and day out. And that's all I've ever tried to do."

> # World changers work hard and work consistently.
>
> •
>
> *Be steadfast, immovable,*
> *always abounding*
> *in the work of the Lord,*
> *knowing that your toil is*
> *not in vain in the Lord.*
>
> 1 Corinthians 15:58 NASB

Cal's brother, Billy, claims that Cal broke Lou Gehrig's record because he could break it. Cal added on behalf of his father, "and because I could, I should."[73]

JACKIE ROBINSON
(1919-1972)

❧

"Baseball's Civil Rights Legend"

"I never cared about acceptance as much as I cared about respect." That was the way Jackie Robinson summed up his baseball career in his autobiography, *I Never Had It Made*.

Initially, baseball in America was integrated. But by 1892, as segregation grew deep roots in the South, African Americans were no longer welcome in organized baseball. They formed separate leagues . . . until 1947, when Jackie Robinson, the grandson of a slave, battered at that barrier.

Robinson's early years didn't give indication of his later greatness. He became associated with a gang as a teenager, and although he finished high school and Pasadena Junior College, he dropped out of UCLA just months before graduation. He was inducted into the United States Army but was honorably discharged after being court-martialed in a race-related incident.

Nevertheless, Robinson also had a reputation for being an outstanding all-around athlete and an intelligent person who came from a fine family. His record at the Kansas City Monarchs, a Negro League team, was excellent. Very few realized that one reason for the difference was Jackie Robinson's newfound faith in Jesus Christ.

Baseball scout Clyde Sukeforth took the chance of bringing him to the attention of Dodger leader Branch Rickey, a man who was not only willing, but also eager to see the color barrier removed from baseball. Rickey outlined the troubles that were likely to erupt if he signed Robinson. Jackie asked, "Mr. Rickey, do you want a Negro who's afraid to fight back?"

Rickey replied, "I want a ballplayer with guts enough not to fight back." Rickey also loaned Robinson *The Life of Christ* by Giovanni Papini and reminded him that Jesus called us to turn the other cheek and not to resist evil.

Robinson agreed, "If you want to take this gamble, I will promise you there will be no incident."

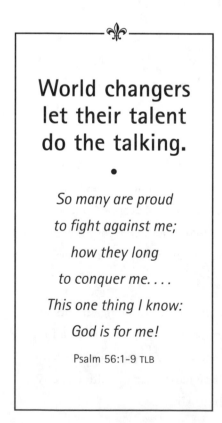

World changers let their talk do the talking.

•

*So many are proud
to fight against me;
how they long
to conquer me. . . .
This one thing I know:
God is for me!*

Psalm 56:1-9 TLB

And there wasn't. Even though he was rejected by some of his teammates and was the target of hate letters, death threats, and unsportsmanlike conduct from opposing team members, Robinson let his bat and glove do the talking. He remained silent through his first two seasons in the minor leagues. In 1947, at the end of his first season in the major leagues, he was selected National League Rookie of the Year. Two years later, he won the National League's Most Valuable Player Award.

Robinson not only opened the way for other black baseball players, but he also became an inspiration to blacks nationwide.

They regarded him as a symbol that other barriers related to color might be removed. In 1949, Rickey said to him, "Jackie, you're on your own now. You can be yourself now." And with that release from his promise to Rickey, Robinson did begin to speak. He testified before the House Un-American Activities Committee on racial matters, and in 1953, he took a personally bold step in integrating the dining rooms of major hotels in Cincinnati and St. Louis. His public statements became noted for intelligence, humor, and a willingness to understand and forgive, as Jesus did.

In his career, Robinson played in six World Series and was inducted into baseball's Hall of Fame in 1962. Throughout his career, he openly maintained "the most luxurious possession, the richest treasure anybody has—his personal dignity."[74]

WILL ROGERS

(1879-1935)

"America's Humble Humorist"

Will Rogers seemed to have been roping and riding all of his life. Not long after he learned to walk, he was riding a pony. When he was a toddler, a ranch hand showed Will how to throw a rope, and Will was soon roping everything in sight, even his mother.

After his mother died when he was only ten years old, Will was given a beautiful buckskin pony named Comanche to help him with his grief. His father encouraged him to ride hard and help with the ranch work. The harder Will worked, the better he felt, and the better he became at riding and roping. After finishing his education at Kemper Military School in Missouri, Will took a job in Texas as a horse wrangler, worked the family ranch in Oklahoma for a while, and eventually worked on ranches in Argentina and South Africa.

It was while he was in South Africa that he became part of Texas Jack's Wild West Show and became billed as "The Cherokee Kid" because of his part-Indian background. When he heard about an American circus touring through Australia and New Zealand, he traveled to New Zealand to be part of the troupe, riding and roping, and eventually he earned enough money to pay for a ticket back to the United States. For a while, he ran the family ranch, but on weekends, he entered roping contests, and again, he left the ranch to perform at the 1904 World's Fair in St. Louis in a wild west show and never returned. After the fair, he performed daily in a Chicago theater and then was given the opportunity to go to New York City with Colonel Mulhall's Wild West Show.

When Will roped a wild runaway steer at the opening night of the show in Madison Square Garden, he became an overnight celebrity with a front-page headline, "Indian Cowboy's Quickness Prevents Harm." He soon was in demand all over the city, where he charmed audiences with his rope tricks and the stories and jokes he told in a slow cowboy drawl. In 1919, he was given the lead role in a silent movie, and audiences loved him on the movie screen as much as they did in the theater. Will and his wife, Betty, moved to California with their children, and Will bought a ranch north of Hollywood, continued to make movies, and added a weekly newspaper column to his work load. By 1928, he was arguably the best-liked person in America. For his part, he said, "I never met a man I didn't like." He seemed to thrive on a busy schedule. As he once told his wife, "Years crammed full of living—that's what I like."

During the drought years of the 1930s, Will organized benefit performances to help many of the farm families who were in need. He raised more than $225,000 in eighteen days while visiting fifty cities and towns in Texas, Arkansas, and Oklahoma. He

World changers extend themselves to others in need.

•

Give, and it shall be given unto you; good measure, pressed down, and shaken together, and running over, shall men give into your bosom. For with the same measure that ye mete withal it shall be measured to you again.

Luke 6:38 KJV

asked that part of the money he raised be set aside for the Cherokee people in Oklahoma who were also victims of the "dust bowl."

Will Rogers was killed in a plane crash while traveling with famous pilot Wiley Post on a trip to Alaska in 1935. Always known for his modesty, Rogers once said, "Shucks, I was just an old cowhand that had a little luck. Why all this here fuss about me?"[75]

WILMA RUDOLPH
(1940–1994)

❧

"She Overcame Overwhelming Odds"

Few people would argue that the most popular person at the 1960 Olympics in Rome was Wilma Rudoph, a shy twenty-year-old who was overwhelmed by the crowds that lined the streets shouting, "Vil-ma! Vil-ma!" Even to think that Wilma Rudolph ever made it to Rome was astonishing.

Born the twentieth of twenty-two children to a tobacco plant worker in Tennessee, Wilma found life as a poor Southern black girl was not enough of a challenge. She also had a multitude of childhood illnesses including pneumonia, scarlet fever, and polio. Her left leg was paralyzed when she was four years old. Wilma later said, "The doctors told me I would never walk, but my mother told me I would, so I believed my mother." Wilma's mother made countless sacrifices to get Wilma the medical treatment she needed, and for two years, family members took turns massaging her leg four times daily. By age six, Wilma could walk with a brace, and soon after, she graduated to an orthopedic high-top shoe. At age eleven she was able to walk unaided, and at thirteen, she tried out for the school's basketball team. At fifteen, she was All-State.

Wilma always considered running to be "pure enjoyment." Her ability on the track—undefeated in three years of competition—resulted in her breaking several state high school records. She tried out for the United States Olympic team, and when she made it, local merchants banded together to give her new clothes and luggage for her first trip by airplane . . . to Australia. She brought home a bronze medal for her part in the 4x100 relay and that same year, enrolled at Tennessee A&I to run full-time for the "Tigerbelles." Illness and injury struck again, and for two years, Wilma missed most of her track dates. She was determined, however, to make the 1960 Olympics. Even though she had the flu during the trials, she set a world record in the 200 meters and was part of a relay team that won both 100- and 200-meter relays.

Once in Rome, Wilma won her first race, the 100-meter dash, and set a world record. Her second gold was in the 200-meter run. The 400-meter race was more difficult. A mistake was made as the baton was passed to Wilma, and the poor pass allowed the German team to move into first place. Wilma ran with long graceful strides and overtook her German opponent and crossed the finish line a full three yards in the lead. Her run electrified the crowd, and overnight she was heralded around the world as the fastest woman in history.

> ❧
>
> # World changers never back down from a challenge that is worthy of pursuit.
>
> •
>
> *Be brave, stouthearted and courageous. Yes, wait and he will help you.*
>
> Psalm 27:14 TLB

Olympic victories brought invitations to speak around the world, a thought that scared her far more than any track competition. She rose to the challenge, however, and whenever possible, she used her fame to help advance the cause of civil rights.

After being named the most outstanding female athlete in the world, Wilma retired from running. She generously signed her last pair of track shoes and gave them to a boy who asked for an autograph. She then pursued a career as a second-grade teacher and high-school track coach. She established a foundation to help young athletes, and until her death, she was a role model for millions of young black women.[76]

JONAS SALK
(1914–1995)

❧

"He Developed the Polio Vaccine"

When Jonas Salk was born, polio was one of the great cripplers and killers in the world. A dreaded disease that struck suddenly and without warning, polio was contracted by tens of thousands of Americans each year. Many died, and most were unable to walk because the disease created painful paralysis and deterioration of muscles and nerves. Fear gripped any household in which a child complained of a stiff neck or leg pain during the summer months.

As a boy, Jonas was not very interested in science. He preferred baseball and comic books. He did well in school, however, and was admitted to City College of New York when he was only fifteen years old. He decided to become a lawyer and began to take courses to prepare himself for law school. Solely to broaden his background, he enrolled in science courses. He became fascinated by his biology course and soon after, abandoned his pursuit of law. He eventually entered New York University's medical school, where he embarked on research to develop a vaccine for influenza.

It was during his studies with the noted virologist Thomas Francis Jr. that Salk became obsessed with the idea of ending polio's reign of terror. At the University of Pittsburgh, he established a laboratory devoted solely to finding a polio vaccine. His colleagues were astounded by his night-and-day efforts—he often worked twenty hours a day, seven days a week, trying one serum after another. Salk reasoned, simply, that if he worked long enough, one of his formulas would prove successful. He also felt compelled by the growing need for a vaccine—in 1952 alone, more than 57,000 people contracted the disease, and of these, more than 3,300 died.

Salk's breakthrough came in 1953, when he developed a vaccine using dead polio virus cells to help the body's immune system create antibodies to fight off live virus cells. The serum worked well in animals, but many questioned whether dead polio virus cells should be injected into human beings. To prove his confidence in the new vaccine, Salk injected himself and his children over the objections of government doctors who urged a longer period of animal testing. Salk declared there was no time to waste. For days, Salk and his family watched closely to see if he or his children contracted the disease from the serum. When they did not, others volunteered for injections. By 1954, the vaccine was accepted as effective.

His work paved the way for Dr. Albert Sabin to perfect an oral vaccine that used live samples of the virus. This vaccine was introduced in 1957.

To further efforts to prevent and cure human diseases, Salk founded the Salk Institute for Biological Studies in La Jolla, California. The institute has attracted researchers from around the world, and their research has

> **World changers seek to save lives, even if their efforts mean putting their own lives at risk.**
>
> •
>
> *And let us not lose heart in doing good for in due time we shall reap if we do not grow weary.*
>
> Galatians 6:9 NASB

resulted in major breakthroughs in helping control viral diseases world-wide. Even in his late seventies, Salk worked long hours, hoping to create a serum to stop the spread of AIDS.[77]

OSKAR SCHINDLER
(1908–1974)

❧

"He Was A 'Mystery Of Goodness' In An Evil Time"

Oskar Schindler was not a man that his peers expected to become a hero. To hundreds of Jews facing the Holocaust, however, he was considered a genuinely righteous Gentile. As one Holocaust father said, "He was our father; he was our mother; he was our only faith. He never let us down."

A German industrialist, Schindler recognized that the Nazi occupation of Poland offered a lucrative business opportunity. He established an enamel-goods factory in Krakow and employed Jewish workers from the ghetto. Over time, Schindler began to lavish what he called "unnecessary" food and resources on his workers. As the Nazis made more and more raids on Jewish enclaves, Schindler responded by making the rescue and preservation of "his Jews" his primary purpose in life. He ran his factory simply as a pretext for saving lives. He bargained, bribed, and even gambled to win favor from his Nazi "friends" on numerous occasions. Twice he was arrested by the Gestapo and interrogated. The first time, he faced serious charges of inappropriate behavior with his Jewish employees. Highly placed friends vouched for him and won his release.

Schindler's boldness grew as the atrocities at Auschwitz increased. As Polish factories began to close, he won permission to transfer his entire workforce of 1,100 men, women, and children to a new site in

Czechoslovakia. When the train carrying the women was inadvertently diverted to Auschwitz, Schindler raced to the camp armed with a sack of diamonds and gold to win their rescue. His new factory, supposedly devoted to weapons production, actually produced nothing even though it was guarded by SS troops and run with apparent efficiency. Schindler refused to contribute in any way to the Nazi war effort and risked his life in playing this high-stakes confidence game. He spent his entire savings to keep the factory in operation, all the time managing to convince the Nazis of his industry and good faith.

Within hours of the armistice, Schindler and his wife fled from Czechoslovakia, disguised in the uniforms of camp inmates, to avoid being captured and killed as German industrialists in the nation that had suffered under German rule. The men and women he had saved presented him with a ring inscribed with words from the Talmud: "He who saves one life saves the entire world."

Those who knew Schindler saw little reason for him to have done what he did. He was not a religious man, but rather, had a reputation as an opportunist, profiteer, gambler, drinker, and faithless husband. It is perhaps his exterior reputation that was his best cover for his many acts of virtue and goodness toward the Jews.

> **A genuine desire to change the world flows from a heart that seeks the good of others.**
>
> •
>
> *A life of doing right is the wisest life there is.*
>
> Proverbs 4:11 TLB

Schindler survived the postwar chaos but was impoverished by his wartime enterprise. When he died in 1974, he was buried, according to his request, in Jerusalem. He was inducted into the list of the Righteous Gentiles in Israel at the Holocaust memorial in Jerusalem.[78]

CHARLES SCHULZ
(1922–2000)

❧

"America's Beloved Cartoonist"

Charles Schulz found a different kind of pulpit for preaching about God's love, exposing the foibles of human nature, and pointing toward the absolutes of God's righteousness: the comic strip. His Peanuts strip, which debuted in 1950, ran in 2,600 newspapers in seventy-five nations. He often used the strip to quote Bible verses or to reinforce the spiritual meaning of Christian holidays, all with a tone of gentle humor and a child's-eye view of the foibles of human nature.

After he saw a "Do you like to draw?" ad, Schulz studied art. He served in the Army during World War II. After the war, he began lettering for a church comic book. He taught art and sold his cartoons to *Saturday Evening Post* magazine. He developed the *Li'l Folks* strip for the St. Paul Pioneer Press in 1947. The strip was sold to a syndicate in 1950, and the name was changed to *Peanuts*. Over the years, a host of spin-off products were developed and licensed, including a series of television programs, numerous books, and a musical, *You're a Good Man, Charlie Brown*.

The *Peanuts* strip was Schulz's lifetime work for nearly fifty years. The characters changed little during that time. Charlie Brown still looked for a winning ball game from the pitcher's mound and saw many reasons to give a "Good grief!" comment on life. Lucy still gave sharp-tongued advice for a nickel at a lemonade stand. Linus still looked for the Great Pumpkin and carried a blanket for comfort. Snoopy, the typewriting beagle, still took World War I flights of fantasy as the archenemy of the Red Baron.

An intensely private man, Schulz nevertheless had international fame. He was devoted to his wife, Jeanne, and children Amy, Jill, and Craig. In later years, he enjoyed playing ice hockey at the Redwood Empire Ice Arena in his home city of Santa Rose, and sipping coffee with friends and fellow players at the Warm Puppy snack bar at the rink. He opted to retire his well-loved comic strip as he battled colon cancer so he could focus his energy on family and friends without the pressures of a daily deadline. Those who knew him well recalled that he worked every day and "never ran out of ideas."

Comic art's highest award, the Reuben Award, Schulz won in both 1955 and 1964. In 1978, he was named International Cartoonist of the Year, an award voted by 700 of his comic-artist peers around the world. He had already been selected for a lifetime achievement award by the National Cartoonists Society before his death.

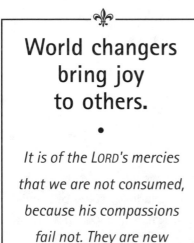

World changers bring joy to others.

•

It is of the LORD's mercies that we are not consumed, because his compassions fail not. They are new every morning: great is thy faithfulness.

Lamentations 3:22–23 KJV

Schulz died the evening before his final strip was to run. His "Dear Friends" strip showing all of the Peanuts' characters, became not only a message of thanks to his friends for their support, but also his epitaph. He once said of his work, "Why do musicians compose symphonies and poets write poems? They do it because life wouldn't have any meaning for them if they didn't. That's why I draw cartoons. It's my life."

A fellow cartoonist said after Schulz's death, "In a couple of centuries when people talk of American artists, he'll be one of the few remembered. And when they talk about comic strips, probably his will be the only one ever mentioned."[79]

ALBERT SCHWEITZER

(1875–1965)

⚜

"Jungle Doctor And International Statesman"

"Absurd," "insane," and "ridiculous" is how Albert's friends described his decision to quit his job as principal of a theological college and study medicine in preparation for work in Africa. For years, however, Albert had dreamed of devoting himself to the "direct service of humanity." He later said that it was after reading a missionary magazine article titled "The Needs of the Congo Mission" that "I quietly began my work. My search was over." As he studied medicine, Albert preached on Sundays, lectured on weekdays, and gave organ recitals across Europe. He was an expert organist and a leading authority on Bach's music. He wrote a book about Bach and also wrote *The Quest for the Historical Jesus.* To stay awake while studying, he often read with his feet in cold water.

Albert Schweitzer passed his medical exams in 1911, then did a year of medical internship, and wrote a dissertation on the medical and mental aspects of Jesus' life. He added his M.D. to degrees he held in religion and philosophy. To raise money to go to Africa, he gave a series of organ concerts and also gratefully received contributions given to him by professors and former students. On Good Friday, 1913, he and his wife said good-bye to family and friends and made their way to Lambaréné, French Africa (Gabon) near the equator. They brought with them seventy boxes of equipment and supplies Schweitzer had assembled. He set up a consulting room in an old henhouse and began to see patients with a wide variety of ailments: swamp fever, malaria, leprosy, rheumatism, open sores, sleeping sickness, dysentery, and the occasional hippopotamus mauling. His wife, Helene, was his nurse, and Joseph Azvawami, a native who spoke eight dialects, was his interpreter. In the evenings, Schweitzer relaxed by playing a small piano-organ his European friends built and sent to him. On Sundays he preached at the hospital.

During World War I, the Schweitzers were made prisoners in their home since they were Germans living in French territory. Schweitzer still saw patients, but his workload was less strenuous, so he wrote the first in a series of books titled *The Philosophy of Civilization.* The Schweitzers were later transported to a prison camp in France, and were ultimately exchanged for French prisoners in German camps. Once again, he found himself in Strasbourg, this time as a doctor.

After World War I, the Schweitzers made several trips between Africa and Europe—in Africa he worked as a physician; in Europe he gave recitals, wrote extensively, and lectured to raise money and recruit other physicians. During World War II, he remained in Africa, keeping his hospital open even in times of short supply and nearby battles. He became known as an authority on two fronts: African medical needs and a philosophy that every person should serve others. He said, "What the world lacks most is men who occupy themselves with the needs of other men. In this unselfish labor a blessing falls on both the helper and the helped. . . . Our greatest mistake as individuals is that we walk through life with closed eyes and do not notice our chances. . . . Wherever a man turns he can find someone who needs him."[80]

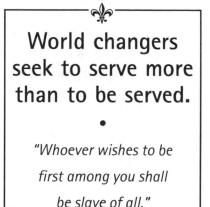

World changers seek to serve more than to be served.

•

"Whoever wishes to be first among you shall be slave of all."

Mark 10:44 NASB

SEQUOYAH
(1770's–1843)

❧

"He Gave Reading And Writing To The Cherokees"

Sequoyah was born at the Cherokee village of Tuskegee in the Smoky Mountains. His mother was from a noble Cherokee family, the Red Paint clan, known for their knowledge of Cherokee history. His father was believed to be Nathaniel Gist, a hunter, explorer, trader, and friend of George Washington. Gist left the Cherokees about the time Sequoyah was born, so the young "half-breed" never knew his father.

When he was born, Sequoyah was actually given the name Tsi-kwa'ya (The Sparrow); but as he grew older, he was visibly lame in one leg, and he was renamed Sequoyah, which means "The Lame One." To the English, he was called George Guess.

As a boy, Sequoyah enjoyed sitting alone in the woods and drawing rather than playing ceremonial ball games or preparing for war. He enjoyed building furniture and small buildings. When he was about twenty, he began working with silver and was soon recognized as a skilled silversmith. His work was often decorated with designs of animals and birds. He traveled throughout the Carolinas, Georgia, and Alabama selling his work. He eventually settled in Alabama and worked as a highly skilled blacksmith.

When the Creek Indian War began, Sequoyah joined the United States Army and fought under Andrew Jackson at the Battle of Horseshoe Bend. Several years earlier, Sequoyah had discovered what he called "talking leaves"—pieces of paper with written words. While in the army, he began to think how much he desired to send messages to his family, but at the time, the Cherokees had no written language. He tried to create an alphabet of picture symbols for Cherokee words but realized that was impractical.

After the war, he spent twelve years listening to the Cherokee language and finally isolated eighty-six separate syllable sounds. He designed a character for each of them—some were English letters, others Greek and Hebrew, and still others original. He became the only person known to have developed a complete writing system. Sequoyah's system was a "syllabary," which reflects syllable sounds rather than individual letters. The system was so logical and easy to learn that most of his students learned it in just a few days.

Initially, many of Sequoyah's own neighbors and friends thought he had gone mad or had fallen under an evil spell. Sequoyah left his village and continued his work in an old cabin several miles from the gossip and scorn. He eventually traveled with his youngest child, Ah-yoka to Arkansas. Ah-yoka was his first student and was a key figure in proving to Chief John Ross, head of the Cherokee council, that the syllabary was useful. By 1822, Sequoyah had taught hundreds of Cherokees to read and write. By 1825, the New Testament had been translated into the new language.

> **World changers are motivated from within and refuse to be discouraged by criticism or external factors.**
>
> •
>
> *My heart overflows with a good theme . . . My tongue is the pen of a ready writer.*
>
> Psalm 45:1 NASB

In 1829, Sequoyah moved to Indian Territory, now Oklahoma, where he raised livestock and sold salt. He died on a journey to Mexico in search of Cherokee people to whom he might teach his syllabary. In tribute to his work, scientist Stephen Endlicher named the huge redwood trees in California after him, and in 1890, Sequoia National Park was created.[81]

AMANDA SMITH

(1837-1915)

⚜

"Although Born A Slave, She Preached On Four Continents"

Amanda Smith's life was largely one of overcoming. Her father, Samuel Berry, was a slave who worked for years at night, after long days of field labor, to make brooms and husk mats to pay for freedom for himself, his wife, and his five children.

She taught herself to read by cutting out large letters from newspapers and asking her mother to make them into words. At age thirteen, with only three and a half months of formal schooling, she went to work near York, Pennsylvania, where she worked as the servant of a widow with five children. While there, she attended a revival service at the Methodist Episcopal Church and resolved she would "be the Lord's and live for Him."

As a cook and a washerwoman, she worked hard to support herself and her daughter after her husband was killed in the Civil War. Prayer became a way of life for her as she trusted God for shoes, the money to buy her sister's freedom, and food for her family. She also became well known for her beautiful voice, and as a result, opportunities to evangelize in the South and West began to open up for her. Everywhere she traveled, she wore a plain poke bonnet and a brown or black Quaker wrapper, and she carried her own carpetbag suitcase.

In 1876, she was invited to speak and sing in England, and although she was afraid of going to England and afraid of the ocean, she went, her way provided by friends who had given gifts so generous she was able to travel in a first-class cabin. The captain invited her to conduct religious services on board, and she later said modestly, "The Lord helped me to speak, sing, and pray." The passengers quickly spread word of her, and she received invitations to speak that kept her in meetings for a year and a half in England and Scotland.

During her stay in England, she accepted an invitation to visit India, and again, she prayed and received not only adequate financing, but also sufficient money to pay for her daughter's schooling in America. She spent nineteen months evangelizing in several cities in India. After a two-month return to England, she traveled to Liberia and remained there for eight years. She organized women's and men's prayer groups, Gospel temperance societies, and children's meetings. While in Africa, she adopted two African children, whom she sent to England for education.

In 1890, she returned to the United States and eventually founded the Amanda Smith Orphans' Home for African American children in a suburb of Chicago. She continued to travel on short mission trips to various nations and gained a reputation as "God's image carved in ebony."

Amanda Smith's motto throughout her life was "without holiness, no man shall see the Lord." She had a practical understanding of holiness and of reliance upon the Lord to supply every need in her life.

> **World changers trust God to help them overcome every obstacle.**
>
> •
>
> *In their faithfulness they sanctified themselves in holiness.*
>
> 2 Chronicles 31:18 NKJV

Her example—as a former slave who rose to worldwide leadership in Christian circles—became an inspiration to thousands of women, both black and white, during the early 1900s.[82]

Aleksandr Solzhenitsyn

(1918)

⚜

"A Voice for Truth"

Aleksandr Isayevich Solzhenitsyn, arguably the greatest Russian writer in the twentieth century, was born a year after the Bolshevik Revolution. His early years were marked by famine and war. He later said his comfort as a child came from a devotional portrait of Jesus Christ that hung in his bedroom. As the only child of a widow, he lived an impoverished life in an inner-city home at Rostov, with no running water or plumbing, and was exposed early to the terrors of Communism. At age ten, Young Pioneers ripped from his neck a cross he had worn since early childhood.

An avid reader, he knew at age nine that he wanted to write. At eighteen, he outlined what became his literary masterpiece, *The Red Wheel*—a multi-novel account of the Revolution—although the first novel in the series, August 1914, was not published until 1971.

In college, Solzhenitsyn became a physics and mathematics major and moved away from his childhood faith. He devoured the works of Lenin, became active in the Young Communist League, and became an ardent Marxist, although he despised Stalin. Then, World War II erupted. Solzhenitsyn enlisted and eventually became an officer in the army. He was arrested in 1945 as a political dissident after letters to his wife and friends, in which he criticized Stalin, were intercepted. His transfers to various prisons and labor camps over an eight-year period became the backdrop for *The Gulag Archipelago, The First Circle,* and *One Day in the Life of Ivan Denisovich.* While at Butyrki prison, he engaged in long debates with two Moscow intellectuals and Christians, and he began to return to his childhood faith.

After his release from prison, he took a job as a teacher, experienced what he called a divine healing of a malignant tumor, and wrote extensively, although secretly. It was the publication of *One Day in the Life of Ivan Denisovich* that thrust him onto the world stage. Again, he became politically suspect, but this time, he fought back with an attack against the KGB and censorship, giving speeches and then disappearing for weeks at a time to write. Microfilms of his works began to be smuggled to the West, where they were published and received with enthusiasm.

In 1974, the Soviet Union labeled him a traitor and allowed him to move to the West with the proviso that he never return to the Soviet Union. In March of 1974, safely in Switzerland, he published a document denouncing Marxism and proclaiming Christianity as "the only living spiritual force capable of undertaking the spiritual healing of Russia."

In July of 1976, he and his family moved to Vermont, where they lived for eighteen years. Every morning, the family gathered for prayer that God might save Russia from Communism, before he embarked on a routine of research and writing for the

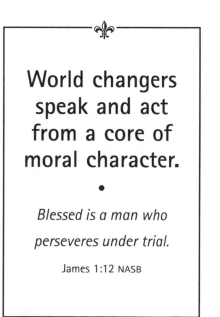

World changers speak and act from a core of moral character.

•

Blessed is a man who perseveres under trial.

James 1:12 NASB

next twelve hours. The family returned to Russia in 1994 after the collapse of Communism.

As a documenter of truth, a brilliant novelist, and a man who stubbornly resisted totalitarianism, Solzhenitsyn is credited to a great extent with bringing about the worldwide collapse of Communism—all from a base of moral power and force of character.[83]

Joni Eareckson Tada
(1950)

❖

"A Profile In Courage"

One July day in 1967, Joni Eareckson dove into the murky waters of Chesapeake Bay, and in less than a second, she felt her head strike something hard, and her body sprawl out of control. Her life was changed forever. Miraculously rescued from the water, she was rushed to a hospital, and after surgery, she awoke to find herself in a Stryker Frame with a broken neck—a diagonal fracture between the fourth and fifth cervical bones of the spine. She was a total quadriplegic.

Joni remained three and a half months in the hospital and was released to what she regarded as an unknown life. She didn't know any paralyzed persons, was told she would not be able to go to college, and faced great physical pain. Her first response was to ask a friend to give her an overdose of pills to end her suffering. Her second response was to live—and living prevailed.

During rehab, Joni began to paint ceramic discs using a paintbrush held in her mouth. Her father, an artist, had encouraged her to draw during her childhood, and she recalled later that it was a simple sketch of a cowboy and horse that was a turning point in her life. Joni also became strong enough in physical rehab to sit in a wheelchair. A little over a year after her accident, she began to attend classes at the university. She took a course in public speaking and focused her speeches on things she knew: how to relate to people with handicaps, what it meant to accept life in a wheelchair, and her experience as a Christian. Deep inside, she sensed God was preparing her for a meaningful life.

Over the years, Joni experimented with different art media and techniques. She gave her artwork to friends and family members as presents. Then, in the early 1970s, a Christian businessman arranged for an exhibit of her work, and her commercial success as an artist began. A book and film were released about her story, television and radio talk programs sought her as a guest, and she became a partner in a Christian bookstore as an outlet for selling her artwork. With each piece of art, she included a brief testimony about her relationship with Christ Jesus.

Joni made a list of those things that were her "heart's desire." They included: "I feel it is time to step out on my own. To step into a new dream. To be a 'doer' of God's Word, I must help others—disabled people with dreams of their own." Out of this desire, Joni founded Joni & Friends, a ministry to bring together Christians and disabled people around the world. The ministry sponsors workshops, publishes counseling letters, and gives financial aid. Joni also served on the president's National Council on Disability. She now hosts her own radio program on more than 900 broadcast outlets worldwide, is married, and is a sought-after speaker. She has written eighteen books, including children's books and books dealing with such diverse issues as euthanasia and Heaven.

She has written, "I don't know what lies ahead. But I do know who I am. I have a dream, and I know where I am going."

> ❧
>
> **World changers endure and overcome life's tragedies in such a way that their experience serves the world.**
>
> •
>
> *"All of you who endure to the end shall be saved."*
>
> Matthew 10:22 TLB

CORRIE TEN BOOM
(1892–1983)

❧

"A Messenger of God's Mercy and Forgiveness"

Corrie ten Boom's early life seemed normal and average in every way. She grew up as one of four children born to a devout Dutch Reformed family that had been watchmakers for generations. The family's business contacts with Jewish suppliers in Germany first alerted the ten Booms to the dangers of Nazism. Willem, Corrie's brother, joined the Dutch underground to help provide escape routes for Jews seeking to leave Germany. Word spread quickly among the Jews that the ten Boom family—which by the time World War II arrived consisted of the father and two unmarried daughters—could be trusted. The hidden passages and attic nooks of their three-story house became a sanctuary for hunted Jews.

In 1944, exactly a hundred years after her grandfather began a Christian prayer meeting for the purpose of praying for the Jewish people, Corrie ten Boom, her sister, and her father were arrested by the Gestapo after they were betrayed by a fellow Dutchman who suspected them of being Jewish sympathizers. Amazingly, the Jewish fugitives hidden in their home escaped detection.

Corrie and her sister, Betsy, were imprisoned at Ravensbruck, a notorious women's death camp, and their father languished in a prison cell until he died a few months later. At Ravensbruck, Corrie and Betsy encouraged the women around them to trust God, and at night, they huddled together and read the Bible and prayed aloud to inspire faith in their prisoners. Betsy died on Christmas Day, and Corrie was released soon afterwards through a "clerical error." The remaining women in her age group were exterminated a week after her release.

Calling herself an "old maid in her mid-fifties," Corrie devoted the next thirty-three years of her life to telling the story of God's faithfulness in her time of pain and misery. She traveled to sixty-four nations, telling her story and speaking out against the injustices and anti-Semitism that had caused the Holocaust. Her book, *Tramp for the Lord,* and her autobiography that became a movie, *The Hiding Place,* brought her international notoriety.

One of the most difficult moments of her life was her return to Ravensbruck in 1947. She traveled to Germany to share the Gospel with the German people, telling them that God's love and forgiveness extended to all people, even to those who had actively participated in exterminating the Jews. At the close of the meeting, she found herself face to face with one of the most cruel and despicable guards from Ravensbruck. She later reflected: "It could not have been many seconds that he stood there—hand held out—but to me it seemed hours as I wrestled with the most difficult thing I ever had to do." Then, recognizing that she had to forgive even as Christ had forgiven her, she extended her hand to this man. The experience led her to proclaim to audiences around the world, "Jesus is Victor," and that in Christ, "we can be more than conquerors." She had validated her message of God's mercy and love in her own life.[85]

❧

World changers forgive those who cause them misery.

•

"Love your enemies! Do good to them! . . . Then your reward from heaven will be very great, and you will truly be acting as sons of God"

Luke 6:35 TLB

MOTHER TERESA
(1910–1997)

❖

"She Cheerfully Loved the Unloved"

As a little girl, Agnes Gonxha Bojaxhiu grew up in an Albanian family in Macedonia. She loved to sing in the church choir, read, and write poems about her love of God. By the time she was twelve, she firmly believed she was called to religious life, and at age fourteen, she joined a church society for young girls. It was there she first heard about Catholic missionaries. As a senior in high school, she felt drawn to the Loreto order in Bengal, India. She later said, "I decided to leave my home and become a nun, and since then I've never doubted that I've done the right thing. It was the will of God. It was His choice."

After a training period in Loreto Abbey outside Dublin, she sailed to Calcutta, where she lived for a while before going to the convent in Darjeeling. In addition to studying English, she learned Hindi and Bengali, and she was given instruction in teaching. She took her vows and the name Teresa, patron saint of missionaries, in 1931. Her first work was as a teacher at a convent school in Calcutta. She took her final vows in 1937. Although she enjoyed teaching, she longed to help the suffering outside the convent, something forbidden in the Loreto order.

Mother Teresa was the school's principal in 1946, when a massive riot erupted. She literally had to roam Calcutta's streets in search of food for her students. There, she saw many of the 20,000 Calcuttans who were injured or dead. The next month, aboard a train for a retreat in Darjeeling, she experienced what she called "the call within a call" to "leave the convent and help the poor while living among them." The next year, Rome granted her permission to work with the poor in the slums and to start her own order.

Before embarking on her work in 1948, she received basic medical training. As an independent nun, she literally walked the streets of Calcutta looking for ways to give of herself and spent the nights at St. Joseph's. She wrote, "I picked up a man from the street, and he was eaten up alive from worms. Nobody could stand him, and he was smelling so badly. I went to him to clean him, and he asked, 'Why do you do this?' I said, 'Because I love you.'"

Eventually Mother Teresa was joined by other nuns who worked alongside her in the streets and went from house to house asking for donations. The order she established in 1950, The Missionaries of Charity, grew quickly, and in 1965, it was granted papal recognition, which meant she could expand her work outside India. She also established a self-supporting leper community in India, an order for male missionaries, and two associations of "Co-Workers" who vowed to live simply, pray for the suffering, and provide financial support. By 1990, Missionaries of Charity houses numbered 450 in ninety-five nations. In 1979, Mother Teresa received both the Nobel Peace Prize and the Bharat Ratna, India's highest civilian honor.

World changers help those who cannot help themselves.

•

She opens her arms to the poor and extends her hands to the needy.

Proverbs 31:20

She routinely taught those who joined her order to treat each person, no matter how ill, as God's child. She wrote, "Speak tenderly to them. Let there be kindness in your face, in your eyes, in your smile, in the warmth of your greeting. . . . Don't only give your care, but give your heart as well."[86]

MARGARET THATCHER
(1925)

❦

"She Was the First Woman
Prime Minister of Great Britain"

As an eleven-year-old, Margaret gave her speech in clear and measured tones to a competition of music and arts at the Finkin Street Methodist Church. A few minutes later, she took the stage a second time to play a piano solo and a piano duet with her friend Eileen. When the prizes were announced, Margaret stepped forward to receive the silver medal in the junior speech class and the gold medal for her piano duet. A teacher told her how lucky she was to win. Margaret looked her in the eye and replied, "I deserved it."

Success and prizes appeared to come easily to her, but Maragaret Thatcher worked hard to get what she wanted, including her place in England's political arena. When she was asked why she thought she had defeated Edward Heath to become the first woman leader of the Conservative party, she replied, "Merit." It was her answer after winning the prime ministership of Great Britain three successive terms.

Margaret Roberts grew up in an apartment above the grocery store in an agricultural village. She and her family attended the Methodist Church four times on Sunday. She worked two to three hours on homework each night, and her grades in school were superior. On Friday evenings and Saturdays she worked in a shop. She was an avid reader of biographies and books about history and politics. She was the star of the debate team in school.

When she was seventeen Margaret enrolled at Oxford University, and there, she divided her time between her chemistry major and conservative campus politics. She eventually became president of the Oxford University Conservative Association. In that role, she met all the visiting politicians who came to Oxford—and they, in turn, met her. After graduation, she worked as a chemist in a factory that made celluloid and plastic tubing, but her life on weekends was devoted to Conservative party functions.

After Thatcher lost her first two bids for a seat in Parliament, she concentrated on a law degree and became a wife and the mother of twins. She passed the bar exam when her twins were only four months old. In 1959, a Conservative seat opened in the wealthy Finchley district outside London. She was one of 200 politicians who sought to win the seat—and she did. Just days before her thirty-fourth birthday, she became an MP. She held a number of cabinet posts through the following years, serving in social security, housing and land, treasury, fuel and power, and education departments. In 1975, she became leader of the Conservative party, and in 1979, when her party gained control of Parliament, she became the first woman prime minister in England's history.

As prime minister, she became known as the "Iron Lady" for her tough economic policies, her military defense of the Falkland Islands, and her negotiations with the leader of the Soviet Union.

❧

World changers work hard in pursuit of their goals until they accomplish them.

•

You who love the LORD, hate evil!

Psalm 97:10 NKJV

235

As a child, Thatcher's father said to her, "Margaret, never do things just because other people do them. Make up your own mind about what you are going to do and persuade people to go your way." She made that statement the guiding principle of her life.[87]

EDWARD L. TRUDEAU
(1848–1915)

❧

"Life Changes Instead Of A Death Sentence"

"Six months" was the noted physician's prognosis. "Two-thirds of the left lung involved in active tuberculosis process" was the diagnosis.

Edward L. Trudeau, twenty-five years old and himself a medical doctor, had only felt a little tired and had known he was losing weight when he went for a physical exam that day. A second opinion confirmed the diagnosis, and Dr. Trudeau decided that if he only had six months to live, he would take a trip to the Adirondacks to rest and relax in the hunting lodge of a friend. When his doctor warned him that the primitive living conditions would hasten his end, Trudeau answered matter-of-factly, "The end is inevitable."

He kissed his family good-bye and then made his way to the remote cabin by train, boat, and finally by horse-drawn wagon over rough roads. He was so weak from fever, coughing fits, and fatigue when he arrived that he could not climb to the second-floor bedroom. Amazingly, as the days and weeks passed by, Trudeau's fever ended, and his strength returned as he breathed in deeply the mountain's fresh air. With renewed strength, he headed back to New York, but no sooner had he returned home than the fever returned. Again, he bundled his things together and went to spend the winter in the mountains, agreeing with his colleagues that he likely would not live until spring.

Yet once again, his strength returned, and he wrote that he indulged in "snowballing, reading, painting, telegraphing, playing cards, hunting, fishing through the ice for trout." Trudeau began to question, Did tuberculosis need to be a death sentence? Could the tubercular find healing help in clean, fresh air, rest, and careful regimented living? He moved his family to the mountains where they lived for six years. In that time, he regained his health, his weight returned to normal, and his only residual impairment was a shortness of breath.

Trudeau began to dream of opening a camp and hospital with a laboratory and a medical staff that specialized in treating tuberculosis. He began the first sanatorium for the tubercular with only $3,000 and a gift of sixteen acres. He also pursued medical research in a field that many scoffed at; and in 1885, he discovered the tuberculosis bacillus. With that discovery, Trudeau launched a search for a serum that would kill the bacillus without harming the patient. He helped develop such a serum that was particularly effective in the early stages of tuberculosis. As a result of his efforts, literally hundreds of thousands of lives were impacted positively and 386 tuberculosis sanatoriums were established nationwide.

> # World changers often turn their personal suffering into a search for those things that bring benefit to other sufferers.
>
> •
>
> *He said to me, "My grace is sufficient for you, for My strength is made perfect in weakness."*
>
> 2 Corinthians 12:9 NKJV

In spite of Trudeau's efforts, tuberculosis claimed the life of his beloved daughter, and it condemned him personally to years of physical misery and chronic invalidism. Nonetheless he persevered. In writing his life story, he said, "I have learned that the conquest of Fate is not by struggling against it, not by trying to escape from it, but by acquiescence; that it is often through men that we come to know God; that spiritual courage is of a higher type than physical courage; and that it takes a higher type of courage to fight bravely a losing than a winning fight."[88]

HARRIET TUBMAN
(1820 est.–1913)

❧

"The Conductor Of The Underground Railway"

When Harriet was fifteen years old, she was shucking corn with other slaves on the plantation when one of the slaves bolted to escape, and the overseer chased him. Harriet followed. As the overseer caught up with the runaway slave and prepared to whip him, he saw Harriet and asked her help in tying down the slave. She refused. The slave again fled, and Harriet blocked the overseer's path. Angered, he threw a two-pound lead weight at the slave, and it hit Harriet, wounding her on the head. She was in a coma for weeks, lying on a bed of rags in her family's small cabin. She could not walk for months. It was an experience that gave purpose to her life—she was determined to be free.

Harriet married John Tubman, a free Negro, in 1844, and she was determined to escape from the South. She later wrote, "There was one of two things I had a right to, liberty or death; if I could not have one, I would have the other; for no man should take me alive; I should fight for my liberty as long as my strength lasted, and when the time came for me to go, the Lord would let them take me." Harriet finally made her escape in 1849. From her safe position in Philadelphia, working in a hotel washing dishes, she later said, "To this solemn resolution I came. I was free, and [my parents, brothers, and sister] should be free also."

Along the Underground Railroad to Philadelphia, Harriet began to conduct her "family". She said, "I never ran my train off the track, and I never lost a passenger." During her lifetime, she made at least nineteen trips to the South, personally helping more than 300 slaves escape along the "railroad." If slaves became reluctant and desired to return to slavery, she was known to point her revolver at the slave and say, "Move or die!" None of her passengers ever turned back.

By 1854, the woman who was called "the Moses of her people" had a $12,000 bounty on her head. An antislavery colleague noted, "Great fears were entertained for her safety, but she seemed wholly devoid of personal fear. The idea of being captured by slave-hunters or slave-holders seemed never to enter her mind." When her identity became more widely circulated and she no longer was able to work safely in Philadelphia, she moved to St. Catharines, Canada, near Niagara Falls. Her trek to freedom, once a 90-mile journey, became a 500-mile trip. She continued her work in spite of the extra difficulty.

The Union Army in South Carolina employed Tubman in military hospitals and also organized a very successful scouting service at the request of the army. Armed with a rifle, she led one 1863 raid with Colonel Montgomery to free more than 700 slaves on the banks of the Combakee River. She worked for the army without pay or thanks.

World changers share an open acknowledgment that all human beings are valuable and deserve respect.

•

The LORD redeems the soul of His servants, and none of those who take refuge in Him will be condemned.

Psalm 34:22 NASB

After the Civil War, Tubman settled with her parents in Auburn, New York. She dictated her autobiography in 1868 and spent the rest of her life making speeches and fund-raising. Her home became a refuge for many poor blacks who passed through the area looking for work and a home.[89]

WILLIAM TYNDALE
(1494–1536)

❦

"He Gave Us Our English Bible"

Englishman William Tyndale faced a problem. He lived in a nation that had few printers, and those who had presses, produced books poor in quality. Not only were the books of Martin Luther—who advocated the Bible as the source to which all Christians should turn for truth— banned in his nation early in the sixteenth century, but it was illegal for a person to translate the Bible into English.

Tyndale, however, felt compelled to do just that. He had studied Greek and Latin and had read the Scriptures for himself. He was critical of the clergy, especially because "the priests of the country be unlearned" and unable to expound Scripture to the laity. He believed strongly that people should be able to see "the process, order, and meaning" of the Bible for themselves.

And thus, Tyndale left England for Germany in 1524. He said to a learned man as he departed, "If God spare my life, ere many years I will cause a boy that driveth the plough to know more of the Scripture than thou dost."

In Cologne the next year, Tyndale began printing his translation of the New Testament in English. He was stopped by religious authorities and fled to Worms, where in 1526, he finished printing his New Testament in handsome, pocket-sized, highly readable volumes. The books became popular quickly and were smuggled in large quantity to

England. For the first time, people read the words that have since become so popular to English-reading Christians: "A city that is set on a hill cannot be hid . . . No man can serve two masters . . . Ask, and it shall be given you. Seek and ye shall find. Knock and it shall be opened unto you."

The Roman Catholic Church in England felt so threatened by Tyndale's New Testament that a surge of heresy-hunting engulfed England in 1528. Catholics felt the New Testaments represented Protestantism as a whole, and they moved quickly in their attempt to crush the growing tide. Thomas More led the debate, claiming that an understanding of Scripture belonged to the pope and Church hierarchy alone and that the common person was incapable of understanding the Bible without the guidance of the Church. Authorities were sent to track down Tyndale.

They caught up to Tyndale, who was arrested and imprisoned in Brussels in 1535. After sixteen months in prison, he was formally condemned as a heretic and was strangled and burned at the stake.

Prior to his death, however, Tyndale had learned Hebrew while in Germany, and he had subsequently translated and printed the Pentateuch, the first five books of the Old Testament, in English. Others continued the work he had inspired, and the first

> **World changers do whatever is necessary to get God's truth to as many people as possible.**
>
> •
>
> *Since he himself has now been through suffering and temptation, he knows what it is like when we suffer and are tempted, and he is wonderfully able to help us.*
>
> Hebrews 2:18 TLB

complete English Bible was actually produced in 1535, while Tyndale was in prison. Those whom King James assembled in 1611 to prepare the Authorized Version relied heavily upon Tyndale. Nine-tenths of the Authorized Version's New Testament is Tyndale's work as is the first half of the Old Testament. [90]

LECH WALESA
(1943)

❧

"He Led The Movement That Brought Freedom to His People"

Lech Walesa would have preferred a simple life with his wife and children, with time for fishing and hunting wild mushrooms. "Obviously," he once said, "God has other plans for me."

In 1943, when the German army still occupied Poland, Walesa was born. His father died shortly after his release from a Nazi concentration camp. Young Lech grew up in a land controlled by the Soviet army and Joseph Stalin. In 1959, at age sixteen, he left his family farm to attend a trade school in hopes of developing a skill that could land him a decent-paying job in the shipyards along the Baltic Sea. After two years of school and a term of army service, he was hired as an electrician in the shipyard of Gdansk.

Immediately Walesa saw that working conditions for shipyard laborers were less than ideal: long hours, few breaks, and exposure to harsh weather. When Walesa took an objective look at his native Poland—from the farms and businesses in his hometown to the Gdansk docks—he concluded that life for the common Pole was one of misery and powerlessness. He became committed to changing that situation. He later said, "It is a Walesa family trait to be driven." Walesa became a union militant, "never pausing to think what it might cost."

In 1970, when the Polish government raised prices on staple goods without raising workers' wages, Walesa organized a protest, leading shipyard workers in a work stoppage action. Promises were made; the workers went back to the docks; but little changed. Then in 1976, Walesa stood up in a union meeting and denounced the organization for keeping its members powerless and criticized the government for making but failing to keep promises. He put himself on the line as leader and spokesman and was subsequently fired from his job. For years, Walesa was followed by police, harassed, jailed for days without charges, and fired from other jobs he managed to attain.

In 1980, Walesa called for a sit-down strike at the Lenin Shipyard. The government negotiator met with Walesa and reached a compromise in the workers' twenty-one demands, including the establishment of free trade unions. Walesa immediately moved to organize Solidarnosc (Solidarity), the first independent labor organization inside the communist bloc. He began to travel internationally to gain support of his cause. Polish leaders reacted to his increasing popularity by arresting and placing him in solitary confinement and declaring his union illegal.

He was offered the Nobel Peace Prize in 1983 but decided not to leave his country to accept it for fear he would not be allowed to return. For five years, Walesa worked quietly in the background. Then, in 1989, the government found itself in desperate economic

> **World changers are willing to give up their personal desires and private lives for the common good.**
>
> •
>
> *I have drawn you with lovingkindness. Again I will build you, and you will be rebuilt.*
>
> Jeremiah 31:3-4 NASB

and social difficulty. The ruling leader called on Walesa to help turn things around. Solidarity was reinstated; free general elections were called; and on December 9, 1990, Walesa was elected president of Poland, the first freely elected president since World War II.

Walesa once said, "Without my trust and faith in God I would have no hope. My faith in God has been the source of my courage."[91]

Raoul Wallenberg

(1912–unknown)

⚜

"He Saved Thousands Of Hungarian Jews"

Born to a life of privilege as a member of one of Sweden's most distinguished families, Raoul Wallenberg easily could have "sat out" World War II. Instead, he volunteered in the midst of the war for a hazardous diplomatic mission in Budapest.

When Wallenberg arrived in Budapest in July 1944, half a million Jews had already been deported to death camps in Poland. Trains loaded with Jews were leaving Hungary every few days. Under the cover of his diplomatic status, Wallenberg began to distribute Swedish passports to Hungarian Jews, audaciously demanding that the Hungarian authorities respect the protected status of these "subjects" of a neutral state. A few months later, the Nazis took charge of the deportation of Jews, and Wallenberg found himself in a fierce contest with Adolf Eichmann, the overseer of Hitler's "Final Solution." Eichmann was also in Budapest, and he believed the extermination of Hungarian Jewry would be his proudest legacy.

At the time of Eichmann's arrival, 100,000 Jews were left in the ghetto of Budapest. Wallenberg had managed to have about 30,000 of them segregated into a special preserve for "protected foreign nationals." Wallenberg routinely made visits to the train station, shouting his way past the Nazi guards, saying, "I am Wallenberg! I insist that all Swedish citizens be removed from this transport immediately!" Before the guards could react, he would hustle the children and anyone able to wave a piece of paper—even if it was only a driver's license or a library card—onto his waiting trucks.

When he met with Nazi leaders, Wallenberg spoke boldly to them of the fate awaiting them as war criminals, even confronting Eichmann personally at a dinner party. Eichmann responded, "When the Russians come, I know they'll shoot me. I am ready."

The Russian siege of Budapest began in December 1944. Eichmann chose to run, despite his claims to the contrary. Wallenberg chose to remain in Budapest in order to do what he could to protect "his Jews" and to oversee relief work after the armistice. He knew in staying that he was a man "marked" by the Nazis and that his diplomatic cover would be ignored.

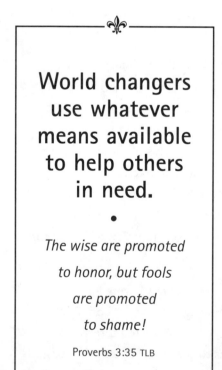

World changers use whatever means available to help others in need.

•

The wise are promoted to honor, but fools are promoted to shame!

Proverbs 3:35 TLB

In January 1945, Wallenberg surrendered to Red Army troops and insisted on being taken to Russian headquarters. He mysteriously disappeared from Hungary and within days, appeared in Moscow where he was held in the infamous Lubianka Prison of the secret police, and for the most part, was treated as a political spy. All inquiries on his behalf were ignored, and the Soviets finally claimed that Wallenberg had died in the battle of Budapest. When pressure was re-exerted in 1950 for an explanation, the Soviets stated he had died of a heart attack in 1947 while in Soviet custody. Reliable witnesses, however, continued to report chance encounters with Wallenberg in prisons throughout the Soviet Union until the late 1960s. His message was routinely the same, "Tell them you met a Swede from Budapest." His exact place, date, and nature of death is not known, and he never knew that tens of thousands of people revere his name and memory.[92]

GEORGE WASHINGTON
(1732-1799)

❦

"He Rose to Lead In Every Situation Presented to Him"

George Washington was a man of varied experiences, many born of crisis. When he was eleven, his father died, and George sought training as a surveyor to help support his family. From age sixteen to nineteen, he traveled the western frontier and managed to save enough of his earnings to purchase several plots of land. His brother secured a position for him in the Virginia militia when he was nineteen. Various conflicts with the French not only gave him battle experience, but also a growing reputation as an able officer. In 1755, under General Braddock, he fought in the battle at Fort Duquesne. He had two horses shot under him, and his coat showed four bullet holes after the battle, but Washington was not wounded. For three years he commanded all of Virginia's forces.

Through the death of his half brother, he inherited Mount Vernon. He added to the estate with his marriage to Martha Dandridge Curtis, a wealthy widow. At age twenty-seven, Washington appeared to be set for a leisurely life as a distinguished landowner who enjoyed hunting, entertaining guests, and serving on his church vestry and in the House of Burgesses.

He was appointed to represent Virginia at the First Continental Congress, and while he took part in no debates, Patrick Henry said of him, "If you speak of solid information and sound judgment,

Colonel Washington is unquestionably the greatest man on the floor." During the Second Congress, he was unanimously voted as commander-in-chief of the Continental forces. He thus became the leader of 14,000 men who had no discipline, no arms, no commissary, and no morale. Through personal perseverance and expert motivational skills, he welded together a loyal army and proved himself a brilliant military tactician. Ironically, Washington would have been denied military service by a modern draft board because he had suffered smallpox, influenza, tubercular pleurisy, dysentery, and malaria. Yet he was never ill during the Revolutionary War.

After the war, Washington returned to Mount Vernon. He was sent by Virginia to the Constitutional Convention in 1787 and later was unanimously elected president. He served two terms. Among his final remarks to the nation in 1796, he said, "Of all the habits that lead to political prosperity, religion and morality are indispensable supports. In vain would men claim the tributes of patriotism who would work to destroy these great pillars of human happiness." He also said, "It is impossible to rightly govern the world without God and the Bible."

Few American presidents have advocated prayer more openly than Washington. He routinely went to his library early each morning for devotions. During his presidency, his secretary found him several times at "work" on his knees with his Bible before him. He gave orders relieving troops as far as possible from duty on Sundays and gave

> **World changers are those who look to God for the help they need.**
>
> •
>
> *Godliness exalts a nation, but sin is a reproach to any people.*
>
> Proverbs 14:34 TLB

them opportunity to attend worship services. He strongly denounced vulgarity and profanity. He was the first to declare a national day of thanksgiving, noting "it is the duty of all nations to acknowledge the providence of Almighty God, to obey His will, to be grateful for His benefits."[93]

James D. Watson and Francis H. C. Crick

(1928) and (1916)

⚜

"They Discovered the Structure Of DNA"

In 1953, a highly competitive race was run: three laboratories were working around the clock to discover the structure of DNA, deoxyribonucleic acid, the "stuff of life" that passes hereditary information from one generation to the next. It is the location of chromosomes on DNA that determines the traits of an individual human being.

The race was won, narrowly, by James D. Watson and Francis H. C. Crick—an American and an Englishman—who were working out of Cavendish Laboratory at the University of Cambridge in England.

The study of genetic codes and genetic influence actually began with Gregor Johann Mendel, an Austrian monk who charted patterns of inherited traits as part of his plant studies at a monastery in 1822. He was the first to scientifically document his efforts to produce hybrid plants in a predictable manner. His work was published in 1866, but it did not receive widespread recognition until 1900. Then, scientists quickly recognized the importance of Mendel's work and began to pursue vigorously the study of heredity, which came to be known as "genetics."

James Watson was born in Chicago. A radio "quiz kid" he graduated from the University of Chicago at age nineteen and received his doctorate at Indiana University at the age of twenty-two. He received a postdoctoral fellowship to conduct biochemistry research of DNA in Copenhagen, and while there, he heard Maurice Wilkins of King's College in London give a lecture that caused him to begin exploring a new avenue of research. He obtained a fellowship to work at the Cavendish Laboratory in 1951. There, his lunchtime conversations with Francis Crick, who was born in Northampton and educated at University College in London, turned into a research partnership.

The two built upon Linus Pauling's research into the helix structure of protein molecules. Watson and Crick concluded that the DNA structure was a double helix—two chains of chromosomes linked in a way that resembled a twisted ladder. Their actual model, which used flat metallic bases and was constructed in a machine shop, was subjected to fellow researchers for confirmation that the model was "stereochemically correct"—atoms and molecules joining up at specific angles—and that it satisfied the existing X-ray data. While various scientists confirmed their findings, Watson took the afternoon off to play tennis. The two lab partners had won the race to resolve DNA's structure, but only by hours.

Fellow researchers were gracious about their victory and the resulting Nobel Prize that they shared with Maurice Wilkins. Linus Pauling traveled to Cambridge to see their model and told reporters that his reaction to their discovery was "one of

> **World changers often work together to achieve in partnership what neither can achieve alone.**
>
> •
>
> *Two are better than one, because they have a good return for their work.*
>
> Ecclesiastes 4:9

genuine thrill." Watson later went on to show that DNA produced RNA, which in turn produced proteins.

The result of Watson and Crick's discovery led to an explosion of scientific theories and research that, in turn, led to innovations we know as genetic mapping and genetic engineering, which many believe will be at the forefront of medicine in the near future.[94]

JOHN WAYNE

(1907–1979)

⚜

"He Was Who He Played"

Many film actors play roles that are unlike their own lives. Not so with Marion Michael Morrison, whom the world came to know as John Wayne. One of the most enduringly popular and successful film stars ever, his movies have been seen by more people and have made more money for their producers than those of any other screen actor. Yet in every film, John Wayne played primarily the role of "John Wayne." The man on the screen was simply an exaggeration of the man in real life.

The real John Wayne could shoot and ride. He learned both skills as a child growing up on a dusty farm covered in cactus and infested with rattlesnakes. Wayne was born in Iowa, but his father, a pharmacist, had moved to California to try his hand at farming. The venture failed, but the family remained in California, settling in a neighborhood near a small film studio that produced quick, cheap Westerns.

Wayne had the size, talent, and desire to be a football player; and as a college student, he earned a football scholarship to the University of Southern California. To earn money for living expenses, he took a position working in the Property Department of Fox Studios. He was assigned to a film directed by John Ford, a notable director. Ford challenged Marion Morrison to tackle him, and he did! Rather than be upset, Ford shook his hand, and the two began a lifelong friendship and working relationship.

A shoulder injury forced Wayne out of football, and Ford gave him small parts and recommended him to other directors. After a couple of major films, Wayne worked for seven disheartening years in small, low-budget Westerns, making more than fifty of them. Then in 1939, he became a star as Ringo in Stagecoach. During the next two decades, he starred as a firefighter, range rider, and World War II hero on screen, always choosing to play a brave American hero.

In his personal life, Wayne was a strong patriot, condemning publicly anything he considered to be un-American. As a producer, Wayne sought only to be a part of stories that showed everything he considered best about America. He nearly went bankrupt producing The Alamo but never was discouraged since he saw it as a patriotic duty and a tribute to American ideals. Even at the height of the Vietnam War, Wayne chose to be part of The Green Berets, a movie that critics and war protesters condemned. Wayne, however, saw the film as a story of American patriotism and strongly defended his role. The next year, 1969, he won an Academy Award for his portrayal of a U.S. marshal in True Grit.

Diagnosed with lung cancer in 1963, John Wayne underwent two major operations in the following year. He battled the disease for fifteen years, remaining enthusiastic about life even as he denounced the 100-a-day cigarette habit that he believed had brought on his illness. He died in 1979. In all,

> ## World changers refuse to work in jobs that are opposed to their ideals.
>
> •
>
> *To do what is right and just is more acceptable to the LORD than sacrifice.*
>
> Proverbs 21:3

Wayne worked as a film actor for forty-eight years, nearly a third of that time with a serious illness. He never gave up on his ideals, his enthusiasm for living, or his career; and he remains one of the most recognizable of all actors of the twentieth century.[95]

JOHN WESLEY
(1703-1791)

❧

"A Giant In The Faith"

John Wesley was born the son of a Church of England clergyman and determined at an early age that he desired to follow in his father's footsteps. He and his brother Charles formed the "Holy Club" at Oxford University—a group of strict, pietistic men who openly protested the low moral standards of the time. At Oxford, he won distinction as a poet, linguist, and classical scholar. He worked nearly a decade at the university as a teacher and was ordained to the priesthood of the Church of England.

In 1735, Wesley traveled to America to preach in the colonies and worked for a time in Georgia. By his own admission, his ministry was marked by a "narrow view of church ceremony and discipline." He placed great emphasis on private confession, assigned penance, and barred from communion those who were not members of his own denomination. He felt a great deal of frustration and disappointment in his work, which was generally lackluster and ineffective.

On his return voyage to England, he was upset by his own conduct during a severe Atlantic storm, during which he was nearly overcome by fear. He was amazed at the strong faith shown by a group of Moravians on board. His restless spirit led him to a little room on Aldersgate Street in London on May 24, 1738, where Martin Luther's

"Preface to St. Paul's Epistle to the Romans" was being read aloud. Wesley later said, "About a quarter before nine, while he was describing the change which God works in the heart through faith in Christ, I felt my heart strangely warmed." Wesley immediately turned to a vigorous evangelistic ministry, especially to the lower classes he had formerly shunned.

He preached at mines and factories, often covering fifty miles and giving three sermons a day. Church officials criticized him, and he was stoned and beaten on a number of occasions by his audiences who were enraged at his teachings against immorality and drunkenness. He was a strong advocate of decency and honesty in public and private life. He taught a "methodical" approach to prayer and good works, fought slavery, gave away nearly everything he earned from writing more than 400 books and pamphlets to combat poverty and unemployment, worked for better prison conditions, and established many hospitals and libraries. Wherever he preached, "societies" were formed to carry on his work, and these, in time, became the basis for the Methodist Church.

World changers give 100 percent.

•

The fruit of the righteous is a tree of life, and he who wins souls is wise.

Proverbs 11:30

Wesley himself was a short, frail man, only 5 feet, 4 inches in height and of weak physique. Nevertheless, he exercised a vigorous ministry for more than fifty years. He traveled an estimated 250,000 miles, mostly on horseback or in a buggy; preached 40,000 sermons; wrote 25 massive volumes on a variety of subjects; and mastered a working knowledge of 10 languages. For much of his ministry he rose at 4 A.M. to pray and travel to his first preaching site, and he regretted greatly when age and increasing frailty forced him to stay in bed as late as 5:30 A.M. At age eighty-six he finally limited himself to preaching two sermons a day.[96]

ELIE WIESEL
(1928)

❧

"A Voice Calling The World To Remembrance"

Elie Wiesel was born in Sighet, a small mostly Jewish town in Romania. His parents were shopkeepers and devout and observant Hasidic Jews. As a child, Wiesel was an eager student of Hebrew, and his parents hoped he would become a rabbi. When he was ten, Wiesel and his family faced the threat of rising Nazism in Germany. Polish immigrants began arriving in his town with tales of horror, and in 1940, his town was transferred to Hungarian rulership. As a teenager, Wiesel sought to escape the thought of war through increasing religious fervor and intense prayer to speed the arrival of Messiah. In 1944, the Germans arrived in Sighet and soon ordered its citizens to wear yellow stars on their clothing, to move into designated ghettos, and eventually to board cattle cars bound for camps in Germany. For Wiesel, the destination was Auschwitz.

For eight months, Wiesel and his father survived slave labor in Auschwitz and then an arduous march to Buchenwald concentration camp. A little more than two months after his arrival at Buchenwald, the camp was liberated. Wiesel's father died at Buchenwald, and his mother and younger sister were victims of the Auschwitz gas chambers. His two elder sisters, Bea and Hilda, survived Auschwitz.

After the war, Wiesel lived in various homes in France, studied, and eventually entered the Sorbonne. To feed himself, he took a job at a weekly Yiddish-language newspaper developed to help promote the establishment of Israel as a nation. In 1949, he traveled to Israel as a correspondent for a French newspaper, and by his return to Paris, he had secured a job as the Paris correspondent for a Hebrew daily paper. He traveled widely as a journalist in the 1950s.

During an interview with Francois Mauriac, a Nobel Prize winner for literature and a devout Christian, Wiesel eventually found himself no longer the interviewer, but the interviewee. Mauriac compelled Wiesel to write of his experience at Auschwitz, and the result was *La Nuit* (Night), which launched Wiesel into international prominence.

In the next decades, Wiesel became a strong voice for the "humanizing" of civilization, writing about Soviet Jewry in *The Jews of Silence,* political activity in *Dawn,* suicide in *The Accident,* insanity in *The Town Beyond the Wall,* faith in *The Gates of the Forest,* and Jewish Zionism in *A Beggar in Jerusalem.* He has written more than thirty-five books, including novels, essays, plays, a cantata, and his memoirs.

Perhaps more than any other person, Wiesel gave a definition to the word "Holocaust." He has championed the cause of Soviet Jews, Biafrans in Nigeria, Misquito Indians in Nicaragua, victims of apartheid in South Africa, Cambodian refugees, and Bosnians in Sarajevo. He was awarded the Nobel Prize for Peace for his advocacy of peace, atonement, and human dignity. In 1987, he established the Elie Wiesel Foundation

> # World changers call us to remember the past in order to help us forge a better future.
>
> •
>
> *By doing right you may silence the ignorance of foolish men.*
>
> 1 Peter 2:15 NASB

for Humanity to bring people together to examine what constitutes hatred or fanaticism. He has continued to call people to remembrance that the human heart has a tremendous capacity for evil, and we must never forget that fact, or we will become victims of it.[97]

WILLIAM WILBERFORCE
(1759-1833)

⚜

"He Brought an End to Slavery in England"

William Wilberforce, the only son of a prosperous merchant family and a popular student at Cambridge, ran for parliament when he was only twenty-one . . . and won! He immediately concentrated on making friends with his fellow politicians, including William Pitt, who at only age twenty-four had been elected prime minister of England. Wilberforce was unable, however, to hold on to his election to the House of Commons. The following two years, 1784-1785, were to become truly life-defining ones for him.

As a young politician, Wilberforce had gained a reputation for consuming enormous dinners and a great deal of wine, as well as being adept at dancing and gambling. He suddenly became thoughtful, brooding, and reserved. He spent long hours discussing religion with Isaac Milner and soon experienced a personal religious conversion. He became determined that his religious beliefs would find expression in political activity. By 1787, Wilberforce had focused on what would become his major concern for much of his political life: the abolition of slavery in England, beginning with the slave trade. He wrote, "As soon as ever I had arrived thus far in my investigation of the slave trade, so enormous, so dreadful, so irremediable did its wickedness appear that my own mind was completely made up for the abolition. A trade founded in iniquity and carried on as this was, must be abolished, let the policy be what it might." He gave his first parliamentary speech for abolition in 1789.

Through the years, various motions proposed by Wilberforce were thwarted or sabotaged by political pressures, his own personal illness, or an ongoing war with France. He embarked on a policy of gradualism, working for incremental changes in slave-trade policies. He amassed great volumes of research, spoke out at every opportunity to decry slavery, organized a boycott of slave-grown sugar, wrote pamphlets that were distributed by those who hated slavery, and continued to press doggedly for reform. Over time, public sentiment for abolition began to grow.

Then, in 1805, the tide began to turn quickly. Wilberforce introduced a bill against slavery. William Grenville became prime minister after the death of William Pitt. Grenville was a strong abolitionist, and he introduced Wilberforce's bill in the House of Lords. After a month-long fight, the bill passed. The same bill was also passed a short while later by the House of Commons by an overwhelming vote of 283 to 16.

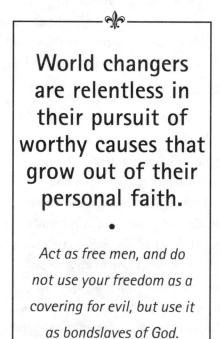

World changers are relentless in their pursuit of worthy causes that grow out of their personal faith.

•

Act as free men, and do not use your freedom as a covering for evil, but use it as bondslaves of God.

1 Peter 2:16 NASB

In the years that followed, England experienced a great spiritual movement. With the outlawing of the slave trade, a new cause began to emerge with Wilberforce as its leader: the total emancipation of slaves. That fight took eighteen more years.

As Wilberforce lay very ill and helpless in July 1833, the "Bill for the Abolition of Slavery" passed in the House of Commons, sounding the final blow for slavery. Wilberforce lived only a few days after hearing the news that his life's work had come to a successful end.[98]

Wilbur and Orville Wright

(1867–1912) and (1871–1948)

❧

"They Gave Human Beings Wings"

In 1903, a famous scientist published an article proving "conclusively" the impossibility of controlled human flight. The vast majority of the world agreed. However, three months after this opinion was voiced, the impossible was achieved by two bicycle makers named Wilbur and Orville Wright. The sons of a preacher, with ancestors who had been pioneer settlers, Wilbur and Orville grew up with adventurous spirits, believing in the impossible. Their mother, Susan Koerner Wright, passed on to her sons her mechanical mind—she was ingenious in inventing household devices. The two brothers read voraciously and attended high school, although they did not graduate. In 1892, when the fad for bicycles was at its peak, they opened a bicycle sales and repair shop. In the winter, they worked at manufacturing their own models of bicycles. The "Wright Special" sold at a bargain price of eighteen dollars!

An article about German Otto Lilienthal's experiments in gliding and his fatal crash turned the brothers' curiosity to aeronautics. They began to read all they could on the subject and focused primarily on the problem of balance. They developed plans for a "passenger kite" that might enable a person to manipulate an airship. Before long, they had built a prototype glider that incorporated their ideas. Their first aircraft, with a wingspan of seventeen and one-half feet, was floated as an unmanned kite at Kitty Hawk in 1900. In 1901, they experimented with a twenty-two-foot-wingspan glider with a weight of ninety-eight pounds, and they surpassed all earlier achievements in gliding.

Back at the Wright Cycle Company that winter, the brothers built a "wind tunnel." They tested more than 200 types of wing surfaces, at various angles, to determine the best ratios between wing curvature, angle, and air pressure or "lift." From these experiments, they revised their craft, and the following year, they added a movable rudder to counteract possible tailspins. They applied for a patent in 1903. In September 1903, they built a plane with a propeller, a forty-foot wing span, and flexible wingtips. It weighed 750 pounds, including pilot. On December 14 and 17, 1903, they made the first power flights known to man—their longest flight was fifty-nine seconds.

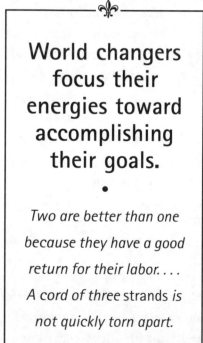

World changers focus their energies toward accomplishing their goals.

•

Two are better than one because they have a good return for their labor. . . . A cord of three strands is not quickly torn apart.

Ecclesiastes 4:9-12 NASB

News of their flights was regarded with great skepticism, even when documentation was supplied. The brothers ignored the pessimism of the critics and turned their attention to making their invention "practical." It wasn't until 1908 at air shows in LeMans, France and Fort Myers, Virginia, that they convinced the general public of their success. Their work was well funded the next year, and the Wright Company was founded. Both brothers continued to work in aeronautical research until their deaths.

Why were the Wright brothers successful when others weren't? Those who have studied their lives have concluded that their success was rooted in their extraordinary teamwork, in their commitment to careful and well-documented experimentation, and in their willingness to use parts already tested and manufactured by others (including their first engines). They were team players focused on a singular goal.[99]

CHUCK YEAGER
(1923)

❦

"He Broke The Sound Barrier"

Chuck Yeager was highly confident that he would be the first person to break the sound barrier during the coming week when he took his wife, Glennis, out horseback riding on Sunday evening. Then disaster seemed to strike. Yeager was thrown from his horse and fractured two ribs. The pain was intense, but he refused to go to the hospital. He knew they would stop him from flying, and he was determined to finish the job he had started years ago at the airbase.

On Monday morning, Glennis drove Chuck to a local doctor who patched him up and told him to rest. That was the last thing on his mind. Despite the fact that he could do very little with his right hand, he drove over to Muroc Base and confided his problem to flight engineer Jack Ridley. He felt he could operate the controls of the aircraft without any problem, but he soon discovered that his right arm didn't have the strength necessary to lift the handle to lock the door of his aircraft. In the cramped cockpit, he could not reach the door with his left hand. Ridley helped come up with a solution. He sawed off a broom, and Yeager used it to push the handle up. He then offered to carry Yeager piggyback out of the plane after he had succeeded in his mission.

At age twenty-four, Yeager had known he was gambling with death every time he took to the sky. He was familiar with danger, however.

During World War II, he had been an ace fighter pilot, flying sixty-four missions against Germany and downing thirteen German aircraft. In 1947, when he began his work with the X-1, supersonic flight was daunting. Planes had literally disintegrated in attempting to break the sound barrier. Most aviation engineers believed no aircraft could fly faster than sound. Early work in the field had been done by private pilots, but these pilots charged higher and higher fees as they approached "Mach 1." The military turned to its own pilots, and Yeager volunteered for the project. The plane he flew, X-1, was dropped from the bomb bay of a B-29 bomber. This allowed the X-1 to use less fuel and fly faster. The plane had no heating and was propelled by four rockets, fired in a sequence.

Early in the morning on October 14, 1947, Yeager made his historic flight. At Mach .88 the buffeting started, and he cut two of his engines and tilted the tail stabilizers. He then refired rocket engine three and continued to climb. The faster he went, the smoother the ride. The needle in his Mach instrument began to flutter, and then it wavered off the scale. Yeager radioed Jack Ridley in the B-29 to say with elation, "Hey Ridley, that Machmeter is acting screwy. It just went off the scale on me."

Ridley responded, "Son, you're imagining things."

Yeager replied in his slow West Virginia drawl, "Must be. I'm still wearing my ears and nothing else fell off, neither." Flying at faster than sound, he didn't even hear the sonic boom his X-1 had generated.

> ❧
>
> # World changers are willing to test the limits of their ability.
>
> •
>
> *That is why I run straight for the finish line; that is why I am like a boxer who does not waste his punches.*
>
> 1 Corinthians 9:26 TEV

Yeager went on to become an astronaut in NASA's space program, but he is still best known in aviation history as the man who flew through the invisible wall that had intimidated so many before him.[100]

JESUS OF NAZARETH
(3 BCE–30 CE estimated)

❦

"The Savior Of All People"

Jesus Christ, to the Christian, is the Hero of all people who make a difference. Only Jesus lived a sinless life. Only Jesus was fully God and fully Man. Only Jesus died a sacrificial death so that those who believe in Him and accept His death as being on their behalf will receive forgiveness of sins, be reconciled to God, and be given eternal life.

No other person has changed history as much as Jesus of Nazareth did. Ralph Waldo Emerson once said, "The name of Jesus is not so much written as plowed into the history of the world." More books have been written about Him than any other person.

His life impacted all sectors of human existence. He wrote no poetry; but Milton, Dante, and scores of the world's finest poets were inspired by Him. He composed no music; but Handel, Haydn, Beethoven, Bach, and Mendelssohn reached their highest perfection when composing hymns, symphonies, and oratorios to His praise. He painted no pictures; but Raphael, Michelangelo, and Leonardo da Vinci were inspired to greatness in painting His life and ministry.

Jesus taught, preached, and healed the sick in active ministry for only three years, whereas many of the world's most noted "philosophers" taught much longer—Socrates for forty years, Plato for fifty, Aristotle for forty. Yet His teachings transcend the impact left by the combined 130 years of teaching by these three men of antiquity. The calendar of the Roman (Western) world was changed to reflect His death, with B.C. meaning "Before Christ" and A.D. referring to "Anno Domini," in the year of the Lord.

His impact on the world is not based upon what He said nearly as much as on who He was and what He did. The divinity of His life is clearly expressed in the "Nicene Creed," perhaps the foremost statement of belief in Jesus as the Savior:

We believe in one Lord, Jesus Christ, the only Son of God, eternally begotten of the Father, God from God, Light from Light, true God from true God, begotten, not made, of one Being with the Father.

Through him all things were made.

For us and for our salvation he came down from heaven: by the power of the Holy Spirit he became incarnate from the Virgin Mary, and was made man.

For our sake he was crucified under Pontius Pilate; he suffered death and was buried.

On the third day he rose again in accordance with the Scriptures; he ascended into heaven and is seated at the right hand of the Father.

He will come again in glory to judge the living and the dead, and his kingdom will have no end.

To those who believe, Jesus is the Ultimate World Changer . . . forever!

•

"Greater love has no one than this, that one lay down his life for his friends."

John 15:13 NASB

In Jesus' own words, "He who believes in me has everlasting life" (John 6:47 NKJV).

How Can You Change the World?

Most of us will not affect the world as dramatically as the people we have just studied. But, we must remember that we do affect the people we come into contact with each day—our acquaintances, friends, neighbors, family, and coworkers. We all have the power to make a positive difference in the lives of others.

Most of us will not conquer nations, but we can conquer our attitudes. We can choose to forgive rather than accuse, to smile rather than frown, to encourage rather than tear down, and to bless rather than curse.

As we daily conquer our attitudes and die to our selfish desires, we are changing the world around us and affecting the lives of those we touch—we are becoming more like Jesus Christ, and He is our ultimate example. We must remember that no one has ever affected the world as much as He has, yet He did not seek fame or fortune. In fact, His only goal on this earth was to lay down His life for us. This excerpt from the poem "One Solitary Life" states it best:

He was born in an obscure village, the child of a peasant. . . . He never wrote a book. He never held an office. He never had a family or owned a home. He didn't go to college. He never lived in a big city. He never traveled 200 miles from the place where he was born. He did none of the things that usually accompany greatness. . . . Twenty centuries have come and gone, and today he is the central figure of the human race and the leader of mankind's progress. All the armies that ever marched, all the navies that ever sailed, all the parliaments that ever sat, all the kings that ever reigned—put together—have not affected the life of man on this earth as much as that one, solitary life.

Be faithful in taking the small steps toward developing a Christlike character, and God will be faithful and enable you to bring about tremendous change in your world.

ACKNOWLEDGMENTS

1 The *Holy Bible.*

2 Milton Lomask, *Exploration GREAT LIVES,* New York: Charles Scribner's Sons, 1988, p. 1-12.

3 John and Elizabeth Sherrill, *God's Smuggler,* 1967; *Christianity Today,* "Smuggling Jesus into Muslim Hearts," October 5, 1988, p. 50-56.

4 Joyce Grosseck and Elizabeth Attwood, *Great Explorers,* Grand Rapids, MI: Gateway Press, Inc., 1988. P. 145-154.

5 Kathleen Krull, *Lives of the Athletes,* NY: Harcourt Brace & Co., 1997, p. 74-77.

6 Milton Cross, *Encyclopedia of the Great Composers and their Music,* NY: Doubleday & Co., 1962, p. 15-31.

7 Steven B. Oates, *A Woman of Valor-Clara Barton & the Civil War,* NY: Macmillan, The Free Press, 1992; Liz Sonneborn, *Clara Barton,* NY: Chelsea House Publishers, Main Line Book Co., 1992.

8 Michael H. Hart, *The 100-A Ranking of the Most Influential Persons in History,* Secaucus, NJ: Citadel Press, 1987, p. 237-240; William Herman, *Hearts Courageous,* NY: E.P. Dutton & Company, 1949, p. 71-82.

9 Michael H. Hart, *The 100-A Ranking of the Most Influential Persons in History,* Secaucus, NY: Citadel Press, 1987, p. 245-247; Paul Lee Tan, *Encyclopedia of 7700 Illustrations,* Dallas, TX: Bible Communications, 1979.

10 Rachel Baker, *The First Woman Doctor,* NY: Scholastic Inc., 1961.

11 Elliott Wright, *Holy Company,* NY: MacMillan Publishers, 1980, p. 130-134; John D. Woodbridge, *Great Leaders of the Christian Church,* Chicago: Moody Press, 1988, 351-354; William Paulsell, *Tough Minds, Tender Hearts,* Mahwah, NJ: Paulist Press, 1990, p. 110-153.

12 Dixon Wecter, *The Hero in America,* NY: Charles Scribner's Sons, 1972, p. 183-189.

13 Russell Freedman, *Teenagers Who Made History,* NY: Holiday House, 1961, p. 105-140.

14 Luciano Bellosi (trans. Geoffrey Webb), *Michelangelo: Painting,* London, Thames and Hudson, 1970; Mac Le Bot, *Michelangelo,* NY: Crown Trade Paperbacks, 1992, and Robin Richmond, *Introducing Michelangelo,* Boston: Little, Brown & Co., 1991; Robert Coughlan, *The World of Michelangelo 1475-1564,* NY: Time, Inc., 1966; Pierluigi de Vecchi, *Michelangelo: The Vatican Frescoes,* NY: Abbeville Press, 1996; and Paul Lee Tan, *Encyclopedia of 7700 Illustrations,* Dallas, TX: Bible Communications, 1979, entry 1503.

15 Paul Lee Tan, *Encyclopedia of 7700 Illustrations,* Dallas, TX: Bible Communications, 1979, entry 4627.

16 Jimmy Carter, *Keeping Faith,* NY: Bantam Books, 1982; Jimmy Carter, *Living Faith,* NY: Times Books/Random House, 1996; Jimmy and Rosalynn Carter, *Everything to Gain,* NY: Random House, 1987; Jimmy Carter, *Talking Peace,* NY: Dutton Children's Books, 1993; Dan Ariail & Cheryl Heckler-Feltz, *The Carpenter's Apprentice,* Minneapolis, MI: Zondervan Publishing House, 1996; Kenneth E. Morris, *Jimmy Carter-American Moralist;* University of Georgia Press, 1996; Caroline Lazo, *Jimmy Carter—On the Road to Peace,*

NJ: Dillon Press, 1996; Ed Slavin, *Jimmy Carter,* NY: Chelsea House Publishers, 1989; and Garland A. Haas, *Jimmy Carter and the Politics of Frustration,* NC: McFarland & Co., 1992.

[17] Sarah K. Bolton, *Lives of Poor Boys Who Became Famous,* NY: Thomas Y. Crowell Company, 1947, 248-261.

[18] Public domain sources and Paul Lee Tan, *Encyclopedia of 7700 Illustrations,* Dallas: Bible Communications, 1979, entry #7696.

[19] Tim Dowley (editor), *More than Conquerors,* Chicago: Moody Press, 1992, p. 265-269.

[20] Paul Lee Tan, *Encyclopedia of 7700 Illustrations,* Dallas, TX: Bible Communications, 1979, entry 1869.

[21] Doris Faber and Harold Faber, *Nature and the Environment GREAT LIVES,* New York: Charles Scribner's Sons, 1991, p. 117-127.

[22] Paul Westman, *Walter Cronkite,* Minneapolis, MN: Dillon Press, 1980.

[23] *The One Year Book of Hymns,* Wheaton, IL: Tyndale House Publishers, 1995, dates Jan. 16, Mar. 12, 14, 18; Apr. 25, May 1,11; June 13,16; Oct. 17; Edith Deen, *Great Women of the Christian Faith,* Uhrichsville, OH: Barbour and Company, 1959, p. 287-288.

[24] Archer Wallace, *In Spite of All,* NY: Abingdon-Cokesbury Press, 1944, p. 59-72; Pamela Search, *Great True Tales of Human Endurance,* London: Arco Publishers Limited, 1957, p. 193-199.

[25] Rebecca Hazell, *People who make a difference-Great Men through the Ages,* NY: Abbeville Press Publishers, 1997, p. 26-31. Also Paul Lee Tan, *Encyclopedia of 7700 Illustrations,* Dallas: Bible Communications, 1979, entry 4624.

[26] Public domain sources and Paul Lee Tan, *Encyclopedia of 7700 Illustrations,* Dallas, TX: Bible Communications, 1979, entries 5198, 2302, and 7693.

[27] Elizabeth Schleicheret, *The Life of Dorothea Dix,* Frederick, MD: Henry Holt and Co., 1992.

[28] E. D. Hirsch, *What Your Fourth Grader Needs to Know,* NY: Doubleday, 1992, p. 35-37.

[29] Rebecca Hazell, *Heroines-Great Women through the Ages,* NY: Abbeville Press, 1996, p. 62-67.

[30] Michael H. Hart, *The 100-A Ranking of the Most Influential Persons in History,* Secaucus, NJ: Citadel Press, 1987, p. 222-225 and Dixon Wecter, *The Hero in America,* NY: Charles Scribner's Sons, 1972, p. 417-419.

[31] Rebecca Hazell, *People who make a difference-Great Men through the Ages,* NY: Abbeville Press Publishers, 1997, p. 62-68. Also, Paul Lee Tan, *Encyclopedia of 7700 Illustrations,* Dallas: Bible Communications, 1979, entries 4608, 5936, and 6145.

[32] William J. Bennett (editor), *The Children's Book of People who make a difference,* NY: Simon & Schuster, 1997, p. 91-96.

[33] Robert Elliot, *Banners of Courage-The Lives of 14 Heroic Men and Women,* New York: Platt & Munk, 1972, 130-141.

[34] Rebecca Hazell, *People who make a difference-Great Men through the Ages,* NY: Abbeville Press Publishers, 1997, 38-43; Paul Lee Tan, *Encyclopedia of 7700 Illustrations,* Dallas, TX: Bible Communications, 1979, entry #4569.

[35] Deborah Hitzeroth and Sharon Heerboth, *The Importance of Galileo Galilei,* San Diego: Lucent Books, 1992; Steve Parker, *Galileo and the Universe,* NY: HarperCollins, 1992; and Peter Sis, *Starry Messenger,* NY: Farrar Straus Biroux, 1996.

[36] Michael D. Cole, *John Glenn-Astronaut and Senator,* Aldershot, England: Enslow Publishers, Inc.,1993.

[37] John Woodbridge (editor), *Ambassadors for Christ,* Chicago: Moody Press, 1994, p. 282-288; David Aikman, *Great Souls,* Nashville: Word Publishing, 1998, p. 1-60.

[38] Public domain sources and Paul Lee Tan, *Encyclopedia of 7700 Illustrations,* 1979, entries #1112, 1872, 2746, and 4137.

[39] Kathlyn Gay and Martin K. Gay, *People who make a difference of Conscience,* Santa Barbara, CA: ABC-CLIO, 1996 and Václav Havel (translated by Paul Wilson), *Summer Meditations,* New York: Alfred A. Knopf, 1992, p. 7, and *The Grolier Library of International Biographies, Political and Military Leaders, Volume 6,* Danbury, CT: Grolier Educational Corp., 1996, p. 101-103.

[40] Charnan Simon, Milton Hershey, New York: Children's Press (Grolier Publishing), 1998.

[41] Kathleen Krull, *Lives of the Athletes,* NY: Harcourt Brace & Company, 1997.

[42] *The Oxford Companion to the Bible* (Bruce M. Metzger and Michael D. Coogan, editors), NY: Oxford University Press, 1993, p. 759-760.

[43] Max L. Christensen, *People who make a difference and Saints-More Stories of People Who Made a Difference,* Louisville, KY: Westminster John Knox Press, 1997, p. 46-57

[44] David Aikman, *Great Souls,* Nashville, TN: Word Publishing, 1998, p. 251-307

[45] Information and quotations from William Herman, *Hearts Courageous,* NY: E.P. Dutton & Company, 1949, p. 193-211

[46] Robert Elliot, *Banners of Courage-The Lives of 14 Heroic Men and Women,* New York: Platt & Munk, 1972, 51-70.

[47] Information from public-domain sources.

[48] Tim Dowley, editor, *More than Conquerors,* Chicago: Moody Press, 1992, p. 118-126.

[49] John Woodbridge, *More than Conquerors,* Chicago: Moody Press, 1992; *The Grolier Library of International Biographies, Athletes Volume 2,* Danbury, CT: Grolier Educational Corp., 1996; and Brian Blandford, *They Took a Stand,* Ventura, CA: Regal Books, 1986.

[50] Russell Shorto, *Abraham Lincoln: To Preserve the Union,* NY: Simon & Schuster, 1991; William H. Herndon and Jesse W. Weik, *Abraham Lincoln: The True Story of a Great Life,* NY: D. Appleton & Co., 1920; Paul M. Angle and Earl Schenck Miers, *The Living Lincoln,* NJ: Rutgers University Press, 1955; and Paul Lee Tan, *Encyclopedia of 7700 Illustrations,* Dallas, TX: Bible Communications, 1979, entries #937 and 4609.

[51] Dixon Wecter, *The Hero in America,* NY: Charles Scribner's Sons, 1972, p.422-435, and quote from Paul Lee Tan, *Encyclopedia of 7700 Illustrations,* Dallas, TX: Bible Communications, 1979, entry #6947.

[52] Milton Lomask, *Exploration GREAT LIVES,* New York: Charles Scribner's Sons, 1988, p. 158-169.

53 Fern G. Brown, *Daisy and the Girl Scouts,* Morton Grove, IL: Albert Whitman & Co., 1996; Kathleen V. Kudlinski, Juliette Gordon Low, *America's First Girl Scout,* Penguin Group, NY: Viking Kestrel, 1988.

54 Michael H. Hart, *The 100-A Ranking of the Most Influential Persons in History,* Secaucus, NJ: Citadel Press, 1987, p. 148-153.

55 Public domain sources.

56 Kathlyn Gay and Martin K. Gay, *People who make a difference of Conscience,* Santa Barbara, CA: ABC-CLIO, 1996, p. 242-245; Jack L. Roberts, *Determined to be Free: Nelson Mandela,* Brookfield, CT: Millbrook Press, 1995, p. 5-45.

57 Helen Clapesattle, *The Mayo Brothers,* Boston: Houghton Mifflin, 1962.

58 Oseola McCarty's *Simple Wisdom for Rich Living,* Marietta, GA: Longstreet Press, 1996; The *New York Times* "All She Has, $150,000, Is Going to a University" by Rick Bragg, August 1995 *(New York Times* Biographical Service); and Nancy Dorman-Hickson, "The Amazing Grace of Mss McCarty," *Southern Living,* February 1998, p. 32-33.

59 Milton Cross, *Encyclopedia of the Great Composers and Their Music,* NY: Doubleday & Co., 1953, p. 471-488; Paul Lee Tan, *Encyclopedia of 7700 Illustrations,* Dallas, TX: Bible Communications, 1979, entry #3721.

60 The *Holy Bible,* Exodus 2-4. The miracle stories of how God brought the people out of Egypt and to Canaan are in Exodus 5-40 and various chapters in the books of Numbers and Deuteronomy.

61 Sally Tolan, *John Muir,* Milwaukee: Gareth Stevens Childrens Books, 1990.

62 Michael H. Hart, *The 100-A Ranking of the Most Influential Persons in History,* Secaucus, NJ: Citadel Press, 1987, p. 41-46.

63 Angela Bull, *Florence Nightingale,* London: Hamish Hamilton (Penguin Books), 1985; Susan Raven, *Women of Achievement,* NY: Harmony Books, 1981, p. 238-240; and Pam Brown, *Florence Nightingale (People Who Have Helped the World series),* Milwaukee, WI:Gareth Stevens Inc., 1989.

64 Kathleen Krull, *Lives of the Athletes,* NY: Harcourt Brace & Co., 1997, p. 74-77; Bert Randolph Sugar, *The Sports 100,* Secaucus, NJ: Citadel Press, 1996, p. 27-31.

65 Rosa Parks (with Gregory J. Reed), *Quiet Strength—The Faith, the Hope, and the Heart of a Woman Who Changed a Nation,* Grand Rapids, MI: Zondervan Publishing House, 1994, p. 11-14, 16-17, 25, 32.

66 Michael H. Hart, *The 100-A Ranking of the Most Influential Persons in History,* Secaucus, NJ: Citadel Press, 1987, 95-98.

67 Victor Hoagland, *The Book of Saints,* NY: Regina Press, 1986, p. 62-64, and Mary Reed Newland, The Saint Book, NY: Seabury Press, 1979, p. 46-49.

68 The *Holy Bible* and public domain sources, especially *The System Bible Study,* Chicago, IL, 1925, p. 250-251.

69 Tim Dowley, editor, *More than Conquerors,* Chicago: Moody Press, 1992, p. 340-343.

70 Philip Brooks, *Extraordinary Jewish Americans,* New York: Grolier Publishing, 1963, p. 220-223.

71 Cass R. Sandak, *The Reagans,* NY: Crestwood House, 1993.

[72] Martin Lee, *Paul Revere,* NY: Franklin Watts, 1987.

"Cal Touches Home," special commemorative booklet published by *The Baltimore Sun,* 1995; Cal Ripken, Jr., and Mike Bryan, *The Only Way I Know,* NY: Viking-Penguin Group, 1997; Harvey Rosenfeld, *Iron Man—the Cal Ripken, Jr., Story,* NY: St. Martin's Press, 1995; and "Cal Ripken Jr. StandsAlone," *Sports Illustrated* (collector's edition), NY: Time, Inc., 1995.

[74] Maury Allen, *Jackie Robinson: A Life Remembered,* NY: Franklin Watts, 1987; Art Rust, Jr. with Mike Marley, *Legends-Conversations with Baseball Greats,* NY: McGraw-Hill Publishing Co., 1989; Jackie Robinson, as told to Alfred Ducket, *I Never Had It Made,* Hopewell, NJ: The Ecco Press, 1995; Karen Mueller Coombs, *Jackie Robinson: Baseball's Civil Rights Legend,* Springfield, NJ: Enslow Publishers, Inc., 1997; and Richard Scoo, *Jackie Robinson,* NY: Chelsea House Publishers, 1987; Chuck Colson, "The Jackie Robinson Story: Baseball's 'Great Experiment,' *Connection Magazine* website. Accessed 1-16-03. www.connectionmagazine.org/archives_old/jrobinson.htm

[75] Peter Anderson, *Will Rogers,* Chicago: Childrens Press, 1956.

[76] Bert Randolph Sugar, *The Sports 100-A Ranking of the Greatest Athletes of All Time,* Secaucus, NJ: Carroll Publishing, Citadel Press, 1996, p. 288-292. Also *Lives of the Athletes,* p. 70-73.

[77] Philip Brooks, *Extraordinary Jewish Americans,* NY: Grolier Publishing, 1963, p. 134-136.

[78] Robert Ellsberg, *All Saints-Daily Reflections on Saints, Prophets, and Witnesses for Our Time,* NY: The Crossroad Publishing Company, 1998, p. 186-187.

[79] Public domain information.

[80] Leonard S. Kenworthy, *Twelve Citizens of the World,* NY: Doubleday & Company, 1912, p. 199-219.

[81] E. Russell Primm III (editor), *Sequoyah-Father of the Cherokee Alphabet,* Chicago: Childrens Press, 1991.

[82] Edith Deen, *Great Women of the Christian Faith,* Uhrichsville, OH: Barbour and Company, 1959, p. 232-239.

[83] David Aikman, *Great Souls: Six Who Changed the Century,* Nashville: Word Publishing, 1998, 125-189.

[84] Joni Eareckson Tada, *Joni Eareckson Tada: Her Story,* NY: Inspirational Press, 1994 (a compilation re-release of *Joni,* 1976, *A Step Further,* 1980, and *Choices . . . Changes,* 1986).

[85] Tim Dowley (editor), *More than Conquerors,* Chicago: Moody Press, 1992, p. 84-89.

[86] Mildred M. Pond, *Mother Teresa-A Life of Charity,* NY: Chelsea Juniors (Chelsea House Publishers), 1992.

[87] Libby Hughes, *Madam Prime Minister-A Biography of Margaret Thatcher,* Minneapolis, MN: Dillon Press, 1989; and Leila Merrell Foster, *Margaret Thatcher-First Woman Prime Minister of Great Britain,* Chicago: Childrens Press, 1990.

[88] Information and quotes from William Herman, *Hearts Courageous,* NY: E.P. Dutton & Company, 1949, p. 123-139.

[89] Susan Raven, *Women of Achievement,* NY: Harmony Books, 1981, p. 87; Bree Burns, *Harriet Tubman and the Fight Against Slavery,* NY: Chelsea House Publishers, Main Line Book Co., 1992.

[90] David Daniell, *William Tyndale, A Biography,* New Haven, CT: Yale University Press, 1994.

[91] Kathlyn Gay and Martin K. Gay, *People who make a difference of Conscience,* Santa Barbara, CA: ABC-CLIO, 1996, p. 407-410; Gerald G. Jampolsky, M.D., *One Person Can Make a Difference,* NY: Bantam Books, 1990, p. 77-95; Tony Kaye, *Lech Walesa,* NY: Chelsea House Publishers, 1989; and Mary Craig, *Lech Walesa,* Milwaukee: Gareth Stevens Children's Books, 1990, p. 12-57.

[92] Robert Ellsberg, *All Saints-Daily Reflections on Saints, Prophets, and Witnesses for Our Time,* NY: The Crossroad Publishing Company, 1998, p. 555-557.

[93] Paul Lee Tan, *Encyclopedia of 7700 Illustrations,* Dallas, TX: Bible Communications, 1979, assorted entries, and William Bennett (ed), *The Children's Book of Virtues,* NY: Simon and Schuster, 1997, p. 16-19, and *World Book Encyclopedia,* Chicago, Roach and Fowler, 1925, volume 10, pages 6199-6206.

[94] Robert H. Curtis, M.D., *Medicine GREAT LIVES,* New York: Charles Scribner's Sons, 1993, p. 250- 260.

[95] Jeremy Pascall, *The Cinema Greats,* East Sussex, England: Wayland Publishers, 1983, p. 19-31.

[96] Max L. Christensen, *People who make a difference and Saints-More Stories of People Who Made a Difference,* Louisville, KY: Westminster John Knox Press, 1997, p. 64-66.

[97] David Aikman, *Great Souls-Six Who Changed the Century,* Nashville: Word Publishing, 1998, p. 308-366.

[98] Charles Turner, *Chosen Vessels,* Ann Arbor, MI: Vine Books/Servant Publications, 1985. Chapter on Wilberforce was written by Charles Colson.

[99] Sarah K. Bolton, *Lives of Poor Boys Who Became Famous,* NY: Thomas Y. Crowell Company, 1947, p. 299-320, and Michael H. Hart, *The 100-A Ranking of the Most Influential Persons in History,* Secaucus, NJ: Citadel Press, 1987, p. 178-183.

[100] Paul Dowswell, *Tales of Real Heroism,* London: Usborne House, 1996, p. 10-13.

[101] The *Holy Bible, The Book of Common Prayer,* "Nicene Creed"; Emerson quote and some facts from Paul Lee Tan, *Encyclopedia of 7700 Illustrations,* Dallas, TX: Bible Communications, 1979, entries #2677-2679

Additional copies of this book and other
titles from Honor Books
are available from your local bookstore.

If you have enjoyed this book, or if it has impacted your life,
we would like to hear from you.

Please contact us at:

Honor Books
An Imprint of Cook Communication Ministries
4050 Lee Vance View
Colorado Springs, CO 89018
www.cookministries.com